THE Grieving Parents *Club*

How to Survive, Cope and Heal After the Death of a Child

Kelly Barbour-Conerty

BESTSELLER IN YOU
PUBLISHING

NOTICE

ISBN: 978-0-9980761-0-2

info@bestsellerinyou.com

www.bestsellerinyou.com

To my beautiful angel, Lexi.

Lexi

TABLE OF CONTENTS

INTRODUCTION

*"Winter is come and gone, but grief
returns with the revolving year."*

– PERCY BYSSHE SHELLEY

I think I screamed, but I couldn't hear it. "We're sorry. We're sorry. There was nothing we could do," they said, all the while trying to avoid eye contact with me. "What do you mean?" I asked. Then, as clinically as possible, one of them broke the news: "She's dead. Your daughter is dead."

I couldn't catch my breath. It was as if someone had sucker-punched me in the gut, and I went into a daze. All I could see were muted objects moving in slow motion. Then, it seemed like everything stopped and went dark.

My beautiful, healthy, and happy-go-lucky 16-year-old daughter, Lexi, whom I'd seen just an hour ago at home before she drove off to meet her friends at a church youth group, had just died.

I knew from the Sheriff's deputy who came to the house just 30 minutes after Lexi left that she had been in a car accident and was taken to the hospital. The hospital would need the health insurance card, so I had it in my hand and ready to go. I was worried, of course, and I expected some bumps and bruises on my child, but not *this*.

Almost as soon as I walked into the emergency room and saw Lexi's body on a cold, steel operating table, people whisked me away from the scene. I ended up pacing slowly along the sidewalk in front of the hospital, not knowing how I got there. I called my family in Texas. When my sister answered, I told her in a fairly calm, almost monotone voice that Lexi had been in a car accident and didn't make it. Then I hung up.

There was no screaming, wailing, sobbing, or yelling. I just kept talking, pacing back and forth, and staring straight ahead. I was numb.

Friends and family, including people from Lexi's church, started showing up in droves upon hearing the news. Most found me sitting slumped over on the grass in front of the ER. I was still in shock when Lexi's boyfriend came, sat beside me, and started to cry. I remember comforting him as best I could, but I still hadn't accepted what was going on. Then someone came out to ask if I wanted to see Lexi before the coroner took her away. "No!" I exclaimed. I didn't want to see my baby girl zipped up into a body bag!

Surely it was all a dream—a nightmare.

No, it was real—as real and painful as it gets.

It was the worst day of my life, but it hadn't dawned on me yet. In the blink of an eye, I'd become the newest member of the *Grieving Parents Club* (sometimes referred to as the "GPC" or "Club"). This was my initiation.

A Completely Different Kind of Club

We choose to join most of the clubs, groups, or other associations in our lives and can almost always leave, quit, or resign from them any time if we wish. People with similar interests or experiences get together because they want to do so and stay for as long as they wish. We like to associate with other people who are like us, and we choose to do so.

The Grieving Parents Club is completely different. It has existed at least since Adam and Eve lost Abel—and will continue as long as humanity does. Members share a similar experience as bereaved parents of a child who has passed away, but membership is dreaded, involuntary, automatic, and permanent. All you can do is learn to function within it. I've been a member for more than ten years already and would give anything to turn back the hands of time and never know what it's like, but that's not going to happen.

Millions of parents are busy leading normal lives with their kids right now. They're making plans, looking forward to watching their children grow up, dream, and achieve so many things. That's a beautiful thing, but at some point many of those loving parents are going to be blindsided by nature, life, fate, karma, God's will, bad luck, or whatever you want to call it, and they're going to join the Club, like I did. Their beloved child is going to die from an accident, illness, criminal act, war, terrorism, suicide, or something else, and they're not going to know what to do or where to turn.

If you're in the Club, you know that experiencing the death of a child during your lifetime is like being transported into another dimension without a return ticket. You can't describe it because it's so horrible. It's completely alien, unfamiliar, and surreal. You feel so incredibly alone and confused, even if you're a person of faith. You may think you're going crazy. Many parents also battle debilitating survivor's guilt, wondering if God or the universe is punishing them in some way, or if they caused or could have prevented the death of their child by doing something differently.

And that's not all. Grieving parents also tend to suffer an identity crisis when so much of who they are or perceive themselves to be is tied up with their role as a mom or a dad of a child who had passed away. It's the ultimate empty nest syndrome, and I think it hits mothers especially hard. Unmoored from normality and faced with darkness, loneliness, guilt, and unanswered questions, they start to doubt their own self-worth and lose confidence in themselves. Many lose faith in others too, including God, and look for something—anything—to numb the intense pain for a little while.

I know parents who have managed to function well to varying degrees after the death of their child, but I know too many others who just couldn't handle it and turned to self-destructive coping mechanisms like addiction (to alcohol or drugs), deep depression, isolation, promiscuity, over-eating, rage, divorce, or even suicide—anything to avoid dealing with reality. The relief is fleeting and illusory, but the damage done to themselves and others is often severe and irreparable.

Without someone to provide a bit of empathy, light and support, the Grieving Parents Club is an incredibly scary and foreboding place where, if you don't move and adapt, you die—physically, spiritually, emotionally, or psychologically. Fortunately, there's a very special and uniquely qualified group of people who can and will guide you in your struggle to survive, cope, and heal, and they're waiting for you right now… in the Clubhouse.

As horrible as the GPC is, membership does offer potentially life-saving benefits if you're smart and strong enough to turn to other Club members —especially old-timers who know you and your child personally—for help. They "get it" and feel your pain in a way that no one else can or does, and they made a world of difference for me in my darkest hours since Lexi died. Maybe *all* the difference. They—and I—can do the same for you. You are not alone, I assure you, and you're not crazy, even if it feels that way.

I saw so many psychiatrists, psychologists, and counsellors after Lexi died. They meant well and some helped a bit (mostly with prescriptions), but none of them ever had to bury a child, so they really had no clue what was going on with me and how to help. The *real* experts on how to survive, cope, and heal after the death of a child were and are other members of the Club, especially the ones who knew me and Lexi personally. Only they knew what to say, how to say it, and what I should do after such a tragic event.

The Club doesn't have an official organization or leadership team, but it doesn't need one. I'm writing this book as an active, long-term member and unofficial representative of the Club, and as Lexi's mom. I'm not a trained therapist, and I don't have all the answers because our grief is highly personal and individualized, but I'm an expert on grieving parents, just the same. I've gained so much knowledge, wisdom, and advice from Club members who came before me, and I'm honored to share it with you. Like many other members, I've lived through the horror "one day at a time," I understand what works and doesn't work, and I'm well-positioned to guide you and others who fall into darkness at any stage of the grieving process.

I've spent many years trying to help other grieving parents function as new members in one way or another. I don't introduce myself to strangers as a member of the Club, of course, but I don't hide it either, and occasionally that information ends up in a newspaper, magazine, website, or television show. So, it's not unusual for someone to contact me and say, "My young daughter just died. Can I ask you how you survive after something like this?" Then I'll have a conversation with them or, if possible, arrange to meet in person sometime. I also offer to check in from time to time if they'd like to talk some more.

Remembering grieving parents and their child on important milestones, like "angel" birthdays, "angel" anniversaries, and holidays, also helps tremendously. Even a simple "Hey, just thinking about you. I know it's going to be tough, but I'm here if you want to talk," or "Hey, I love this photo of your son" can brighten up a dark day. So, I do it whenever I can, and I appreciate it when others do it for me. I also make a point of referring to the departed children of grieving parents in the *present* tense because their memory is very present for any member of the Club.

In addition, since the fall after Lexi's fatal auto accident in 2006, I've dedicated myself to educating high school students, driver's education students, parents, and communities about a subject dear to my heart – safe driving. Lexi was speeding, distracted, and not wearing a seatbelt when she lost control of her car, crashed, and died. I can't change what happened to my daughter, as much as I wish I could, but I can try to prevent the death of other teenagers in traffic accidents and keep their parents out of the Club.

Perhaps it's no surprise that I'm writing this book because I consider myself a communicator. I'm an associate professor of business at Parkland College in Champaign, Illinois, where I communicate with and educate students about business, finance, economics, marketing and management on a daily basis, and I love it. So, after Lexi died, I simply expanded the scope of subjects to include teenage safe driving and grieving parents.

However, I must admit that I was extremely reluctant to write this book for many years and nearly chickened out at the eleventh hour. I knew I had something meaningful to say, but I really didn't want to revisit so many painful memories surrounding Lexi's death. I was crying a lot and not sleeping well. Friends questioned whether I should be doing something that clearly bothered me so much. Then, self-doubt and bitterness began to supersede my desire to help others. "Why would anybody be interested in what I have to say? I'm a nobody." "Why should I make myself miserable? Let other grieving parents figure it out on their own, like I did."

I kept going anyway for several reasons. First, I'm not going to be around forever to help others function within the Club. This book, on the other hand, can serve as kind of an orientation for new members of the Club long after I'm gone. Second, if this book helps even one grieving parent, it was definitely worth it. Third, this book might also help friends and family of Club members better understand and support them in tough times. And last but not least, I want the world to know about my sweet, adorable baby girl, Lexi, and keep her uplifting, magical spirit alive and well.

There's an organization called Families Against Chronic Excessive Speed (Faces4.org) in Naperville, Illinois that creates palm cards with a picture of someone who has died from speeding, along with their name and the date that they died. State police give them to people who are pulled over for speeding, and one of them has Lexi on it. I have tons of these cards and hand them out at high schools. Well, as I was doing it the other day, I looked down and saw the words "Died, June 28, 2006" next to Lexi's photo.

Then it occurred to me: *This* is why I'm so active in the Club, and why I needed to finish writing this book. No parent should ever have to see the word "Died" and a date next to their child's name and picture, and I want to do everything I can do help them if and when it happens.

Lights in the Darkness

This book is for grieving parents. It's about what to do and how to survive, cope, and heal after your child dies and you become a member of the Club. I hope that my thoughts on teenage safe driving will prevent at least some parents from ever joining the Club, but this book is first and foremost for my fellow members in the Club, especially the newest ones.

If you remember nothing else after reading this book, remember this: Other Club members are ready, willing, and able to guide you through your new normal. There are a lot of us in the Clubhouse, including some of the nicest and most caring people you'll ever meet, and we all carry little flashlights, torches, and candles to help you find your way out of the darkness. You will have to walk the path yourself and do it your way, but we'll be there.

Everyone's grief is their own; there is no one-size-fits-all way to grieve. This was *your* child, and you will have to learn how to function, cope, and thrive in a way that works best for you, but we can help you do that in an honest and empathetic way. You will also learn about coping mechanisms and techniques that have worked or not worked for other members at different stages of the grieving process, including what I refer to as:

- Joining the Club
- Facing the Cold, Hard Reality
- Alone Again, Naturally (Surviving the Milestones)
- The Last Damn Bridge
- Keep Moving

We can pinpoint when things are going to happen or are likely to happen and how you're going to feel (more or less). We can reassure you that your feelings and emotions are perfectly normal and acceptable, even when non-members are telling to you to "Get over it," "Move on," or even "Oh well… It's God's will." And we can help you to look ahead, prepare, and steel yourself against foreseeable challenges, especially the ones that are likely to happen more than once.

In that moment of complete darkness, that scary and unfamiliar place, there are many of us who are ready to guide you along the way. You'll soon realize that you're not alone and we're never going to let you be alone. We can't make your journey for you, but we'll do everything we can to help, guide, support, and arm you with the resources you need to find hope and joy, laugh and love again, appreciate the beauty in and around you, make a positive difference in the world, and still honor your child's memory.

On January 31, 2015, the only child of a friend of mine – her beloved son, Nicholas – was killed. He had dreamed of becoming an Oklahoma State Trooper, made it happen to the delight of his very proud mother, and had only been on the squad for a little over a year when he pulled over to help a stranded motorist. As usual, he had the lights on his squad car flashing when he got out to assist the motorist, but some idiot in another car who was speeding, texting, and updating his social-media status apparently didn't notice the flashing lights and plowed into Nicholas. He never had a chance.

My friend was devastated and went to a very dark place for the next year or so. At times, she's considered taking a handful of pills and killing herself. This was her only child, and his death was so senseless. He should not have been killed, and he left behind two small daughters who need their daddy.

How do I know about all this? I know because I'd been doing my best to help her since February 1, 2015, when she got that knock on the door and joined the Club. For a while, I checked on her every day because she was posting status updates on social media about how she was ready to end it all. Naturally, I was worried. So, I'd ask her to tell me about photos of Nicholas and the story behind them if she wanted to, and she usually did.

I also tried to encourage her to start running again. My friend, like me, was an avid runner—we'd enjoyed running crazy marathons and half-marathons and things like that in past—but she'd stopped running completely after her son's death. She'd say, "People think I'm being selfish with my running," but I was like, "I don't care what people say. What do *you* feel like doing today?"

Eventually, she started running again. It was great, and it led to something greater. When she came out of her daze, she decided to do something in her son's honor. She worked to set up a charity for a virtual run, then an actual 5K run, and then a 7.31 mile "Run the Badge" event in honor of her son and his Oklahoma Highway Patrol State Trooper badge number, 731. The proceeds provide scholarships for students in rural, low-income southeastern Oklahoma.

It gave her life meaning again, and it kept her son's badge, picture, and memory alive. She even gave me an honorary bib to wear, with Nicholas's face on it. I wore it on the back of my shirt when I ran the New York City Marathon last year. And, sure enough, when people asked me about it, I had an opportunity to tell them a story about how this young man, father, good person, and only child of a very sweet lady had been killed because somebody was stupid and reckless enough to be texting while speeding on the interstate.

That was just what my friend did. All I could do as a fellow member of the Club was be there to help her figure out how she needed to grieve, and what she needed to do to go on. We're all different. You can ask other people for advice and suggestions, but you have to find something meaningful and constructive to do that helps others and keeps your child's face, voice, story and memory alive. Your life has changed, and there still will be dark times, but you can take steps to give it purpose and passion again.

Ultimately, this book is about hope—about knowing *that there are others in the Clubhouse* who know exactly how you feel and can help you make it through. Those of us who have been members for a while can offer a little light, ideas that helped us to survive, cope and help, and helped us to keep our child's name and memory alive. New members need to know and learn that, even in your grief, it's still OK to smile, laugh, and have fun.

You Are Not Alone

If this book touches or helps you, don't just put it down and keep going it alone through the darkness, no matter how tough, introverted, stubborn, embarrassed, or independent you think you are. We can't help you if you stay in the dark too long because you'll destroy yourself or quit on life. It's too easy to let pain get the better of you, and we've lost too many grieving parents to suicide, addiction, and other self-destructive behaviors already. There's no sense in making a bad situation worse for yourself and others.

Reach out to other members of the Club instead, especially the ones who know you personally or old-timers like me. And if somebody lets you down for any reason—perhaps they're going through a dark period themselves— try again. It's a huge Club. There are plenty of us, and we care about you.

I also invite you to join other grieving parents as part of a larger purpose and community. There are many other resources available for counseling, talking, and understanding how to function as a member of the Club; *The Compassionate Friends* is one such group, and there are other groups you can reach through many churches.

Those resources already serve many people, but they aren't for me. When I have periods of deep pain, darkness or loneliness—yes, it still happens—I prefer to communicate with people who know me, Lexi, and my story, or at least aren't total strangers. That's why I've established The Grieving Parents Club (www.GrievingParentsClub.org) – to do things a little differently. So, if you're a grieving parent who's looking for something a little more intimate—or at least that's what I hope it will be—check out the site and, if you wish, join me. We can work together to fill that need.

This book is just the beginning. Our grief is never-ending—in this life, at least—but it doesn't have to define or break us. We can hold our child's name, face, voice and spirit closer in our memories. We can hold other loved ones closer in our arms. And we can survive, cope and heal with a little help from wise, caring and empathetic members in the Clubhouse.

CHAPTER 1

JUST YOU AND ME, KID

"Let us always meet each other with a smile,
for the smile is the beginning of the love."
– MOTHER THERESA

TEXAS: November 29, 1989 to July 1994

I was a 22-year old from rural, southeastern Oklahoma who had been an undergraduate student at Harvard. I had also been in a long-term relationship with someone who was verbally, mentally, and occasionally physically abusive throughout it, especially toward the end, but I didn't have enough self-confidence to get out at the first signs.

I had to get out of there. So I found some long-lost strength, packed up my little 1979 AMC Spirit that barely got me from Point A to Point B, drove down I-95, and showed up at my parent's house in Texas.

I rented a little apartment of my own initially as I tried to get my bearings and figure things out. I was young, single, and pregnant. My hormones were racing, and I was confused. My educational and career plans had changed radically, and everything was chaotic. As the delivery date moved closer, my grandparents offered to let me to move to another place of theirs in a small town northeast of Dallas, and I did. I also decided to finish up my bachelor's degree at nearby East Texas State University, which is now part of the Texas A&M system.

Lexi was born on a cold day November 29, 1989 in Greenville, Texas. She was late, and huge! I was huge, too, not to mention miserable after an intensely painful labor and delivery. I'd been around children before—I'm the oldest of six kids and almost sixteen years older than my youngest brother—but this was different. I was going to be a single mother, and I was scared.

When she finally came out, my mom called her a little Cherokee Indian. She had black hair like a little Indian baby, and she looked just like my grandma. I named her after a friend of mine at Harvard named Lexi, which is short for Alexandra. The name Lexi fit her better because she was just so little. So, even though her legal name is Alexandra Jane, she was always a Lexi. That was her personality from birth.

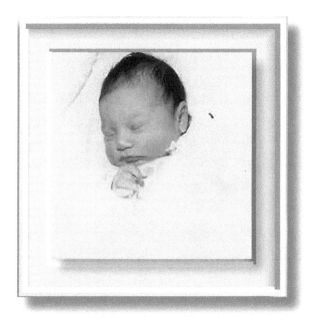

Lexi as a newborn

We spent the next couple of weeks at my parents' house in Fort Worth, Texas while I recovered and recuperated, but we moved back to the little house after Christmas and, for the first time, it was just the two of us.

I started classes at East Texas State in January of 1990 and was able to really focus on cranking out classes because of some scholarships that I'd received based on need and academic achievement. Meanwhile, my grandparents helped out by watching Lexi while I took classes during the day, especially during the first few months. They loved it because they got to hang out with her and spoil her. After a few months of paperwork and approvals, I was able to drop Lexi off at a daycare center on campus for university students, which allowed me to go see her in between classes.

I had a lot of moral support from my family and the university, but it was always just the two of us at nighttime—this little human being and me.

Lexi at 2 years old.

Fortunately, Lexi was a happy baby. She was always laughing and smiling. They say newborns and little babies don't really smile; that it's gas or colic or something like that. But Lexi wasn't one of those colicky, grouchy babies. She was always calm, cheerful, and giggling, no matter what was going on. She adapted quickly.

She was remarkably independent from a very young age as well. She played and shared well with other kids, but she could amuse herself and find things to do on her own anytime. She was fascinated and delighted by so many little things, like the lights and sounds of the car when I put her in her little seat at six months old, and the music of the show *Jeopardy!* when we sat down in front of the TV to watch it.

She also had a naturally beautiful singing voice. By the time she was two years old, she was making up her own lyrics to songs, and she wasn't shy about singing them at the top of her lungs. It was hilarious. Amazingly, my youngest daughter Anastasia (or "Stasia")—who was only 2 years old when Lexi died—did the exact same thing at about the same age, and she sings well, too. Maybe it's a genetic thing, but I can't carry a tune in a bucket.

About the same time, when Lexi was about two, my extended family decided to have a reunion in Albuquerque, New Mexico. Half the family was in Oklahoma and Texas, the other half was in California, so Albuquerque was right in the middle for everyone. My grandparents joined Lexi and me on the flight from Texas.

Once we boarded the plane and took our seats, Lexi kept saying "Hi" and "We're going to Albuquerque" to the flight attendants and everyone else within earshot. She liked the airline cookies too, said so, and before long other passengers were passing their cookies along to the little girl with big brown eyes, dark ringlets, and a sweet southern accent. Then, when we arrived safely at our destination, she kept saying "I flew Shamu" because there was a painting of Shamu, the killer whale, on the side of our plane.

We flew to California the following year, and Lexi made sure to let everyone know that she was going to Disneyland. And, as soon as we arrived, she walked right over to Donald Duck, Mickey Mouse and the other characters, introduced herself, and talked up a storm. She did the same thing with people waiting in line for rides with us, and they reacted in a similar way. They'd smile, laugh and say something like, "Oh, my gosh, what a cute kid."

As for the attractions, she wanted to go on the "It's a Small World" ride over and over again and sing along. She thought the ghosts in the Haunted House were a riot. When they disappeared, she'd say "Where'd they go? Can they come home with us? Will they let them on the airplane?" She enjoyed driving those mini-cars like a crazy person, with me sitting beside her, feeling grown up because she was behind the wheel for the first time. But her favorite thing was animatronic President Abraham Lincoln or "Mr. Lincoln." When she saw him, she was just like, "Wow, that's so cool."

There was another character whom Lexi loved even more than the Disney ones, and I dare not say his name for fear he may somehow resurface. Suffice it to say, he's a big, goofy purple dinosaur. Lexi never missed an episode of his TV show and sang along with him every time. She had t-shirts and sweats, pajamas, a sleeping bag, a hat, a coat, slippers, and sneakers with his picture plastered on them, too. It was like a ride on "It's a Small World" at Disneyland that never ends. These days, I don't even allow his name to be spoken in my house. Can't do it.

When she was three and a half, Lexi performed in her first school play at the daycare center there in East Texas. She had one line, "The cowboys moved the big herds of cattle a long way to the railroads." I remember it well because we practiced a lot before the big show. All of the kids got one line and were asked to come forward and deliver it. When it was Lexi's turn, she walked up there wearing her little paper vest, with her shoulders back and head up, and she didn't yell her line. She enunciated clearly, and the cowboys moved the big herds of cows back to railroad. Then she curtsied proudly. Perfect.

She was the oldest grandchild on my side of the family. When she first started talking, we're pretty sure that she was trying to say "granddaddy" or something like that, but with her cute little Texas accent it came out "Big Daddy." Grandpa became Big Daddy after that.

My mother didn't get a cute nickname from Lexi—she had decided to call herself "Mimi," but Lexi enjoyed going out to the garden with her Mimi. Lexi would point at the flowers and say, "pitty, pitty, flowers." That just tickled my mom to death. Lexi also liked to say "Let's go chopping, Mimi," which meant another fun trip to Walmart!

Lexi and Mimi

My brothers were younger than me (my youngest brother was only about six years older than Lexi), and Lexi would not shy away from roughhousing with them. She was girly with her dresses and all that, but when the boys, her uncles, would wrestle each other or my dad, she was right in there. My dad watched "20,000 Leagues Under the Sea" with Lexi once, and Lexi saw the giant squid come up. After that, whenever she said, "We gotta play giant squid," it was on. She was ready to rumble with her uncles and Big Daddy.

Lexi, Big Daddy, and her uncles

Lexi had a very special relationship with my grandparents (her great-grandparents), too. My granddad had a ranch with cattle and horses, and we had a Shetland pony named "Baby Doll" since I was eight or nine years old. "Frou Frou," who came later, was her foal. They had a great life, doing nothing besides eating most days, and they were old by the time Lexi was two or three years old, but it didn't matter. My granddad would hold Lexi's hand out and let her feed the horses with the food he prepared specially for them.

My granddad taught Lexi to ride Baby Doll and Frou Frou, too. The horses knew who she was, and my granddad or somebody would hold her on the horses in the beginning. I remember one day when my granddad didn't have a rope, so he grabbed jumper cables from the truck and used them instead of a rein. Lexi held onto his arm with one hand and Baby Doll's mane with the other. Baby Doll didn't care. She was a calm, happy 20-year old horse, and she knew she was loved.

Lexi, Dada Harlan, Baby Doll, and FrouFrou

My whole family grew up around horses and cows, and so did Lexi. But feeding them the special feed that my granddaddy mixed up just for Baby Doll and Frou Frou was Lexi's special alone time with her great-grandfather. I could sit in the car, but I was not allowed to intrude on their time. She had a very special relationship with her great grandparents.

Lexi, Dada Harlan, Grami Lois

The black and white picture on the cover of this book was also taken during our years in Texas. We were attending the "Bois d'Arc Bash" carnival in the town square of a little bitty town called Commerce in Northeast Texas, where the university is located. Bois d'Arc trees are everywhere in Commerce.

A photographer from the local weekly Commerce newspaper noticed us sitting there and happened to catch that shot of Lexi looking over at some other people with her face painted while eating her ice cream. It appeared in the paper, and the photographer kindly sent me the prints. I love that photo because it really captured her personality. She made friends so easily. People were attracted to her aura. The timing was perfect

Lexi might be a little shy around strangers at first, but before long she was always the center of attention, performing, posing, pretending, telling jokes (and getting the punch line wrong), singing, laughing, and chatting non-stop. She'd talk about whatever she was doing and thinking, which is why we had a secret code word that everybody had to say before they could pick her up at daycare or take her anywhere else. It was "Gertrude McGillicuddy." She came up with it herself, and it worked like a charm.

Meanwhile, I had a chance to spend the summer of '93 at the University of Michigan, where I was accepted into a program designed to encourage minority graduate students into getting their PhD at the school. While I was up there, I met some people from the University of Illinois and decided to apply to their PhD program in Corporate Finance. I did, and several months later, they accepted me. They offered me a fellowship, too.

I didn't seek a PhD to become a teacher. Teaching was the furthest thing from my mind when I was in my 20's. I didn't want to be a teacher because everybody in my family is a teacher. I didn't want to deal with kids and principals and parents. I didn't dream of landing a husband, having more kids, and a little house with a white picket fence either, at least not back then. I wanted to go the corporate route—to be independently successful, rich, powerful, and all the rest—and this was an opportunity to do it.

Lexi and I had lived in that little house in Greenville, Texas for a long time, but it was time to go. So, after we loaded up our car and a U-Haul with some help from my dad, we drove north to a little apartment in Champaign, Illinois. We didn't know anyone there, other than a few people whom I met recently at the University of Illinois. It was just the two of us, really. I could call my family for support, but we were on our own now.

Lexi was almost five.

ILLINOIS: August 1994 to April 1998

We tried to acclimate to our new surroundings in Illinois, but it took some time because was so different from Texas. When I went to class, Lexi went to the daycare center, but we saw the sights whenever we could and played together in a nice park across the street from where we lived.

January and February of '95 were ridiculously cold in Champaign, Illinois. The wind chill factor was like 80 below zero for a couple days in a row, and I was seriously rethinking my move north. It wasn't worth it. Nothing was worth living in a place that chilly, but Spring came soon enough, the weather improved, and Lexi discovered something else that she loved: *The Mighty Morphin Power Rangers* TV show.

She loved the Pink Ranger so much that she wanted to *be* the pink ranger. One day around that time, I heard that the Power Rangers were coming to Peoria, Illinois, which was about an hour away. We didn't have a lot of money, but I bought some cheap tickets, and we drove over there on a Sunday afternoon. Lexi was thrilled as we sat in the stands of the convention center with a good view of the stage where the Power Rangers were doing their thing.

At one point during the show, Lexi started giggling. I didn't think anything about it because she was always giggling, but then I had an eerie feeling that somebody was watching me, and I looked over my shoulder to find out. The bad minion, the Putty Monster, was right behind me, and I screamed bloody murder. Lexi doubled over laughing and snorting with glee. Naturally, for the next few weeks, she told everyone we met how brave she was when Putty Monster came over, and how it scared her mom and made her scream. She'd say things like, "Hey, did you know a Putty Monster scared my mom? My mom's so silly." She thought it was hilarious.

We traveled a lot together, especially after the first year in Illinois. We'd just get in the car and go on a day trip—maybe find a little motel with an indoor swimming pool or something fun going on out of town. We'd visit family during the summertime, too. So, on the drive down to Texas from Illinois or on the way back, we would stop and see roadside tourist things. My granddad never let us leave Texas without some fried cornbread that he'd just made. He would take old plastic gallon milk jugs and fill them up with water every time he'd go to the farm. You always wanted to make sure that you had water in Texas because of the dry heat.

On one of our trips back to Illinois from Texas, I had a plastic grocery sack full of fried cornbread and a milk jug full of water as we approached the Arkansas border, and it was so hot. We saw a sign for Crater of Diamonds State Park, assumed it must be nearby, and decided to check it out. We drove through little mountain roads for an hour before we finally arrived. It's basically the site of an extinct volcano, and people occasionally find diamonds there. They charge $5 for you to try your luck. So Lexi and I sat in the dirt and dug for diamonds, while eating the corn bread and drinking water out of that plastic jug for about two hours. We didn't find any diamonds, but Lexi was excited to dig up some quartz and all sorts of other things.

We also looked for opportunities to cross state lines as much as possible because Lexi always wanted to one-up or out-do her uncles (my brothers) and one of those ways was to visit more States than they did. So, during one of our trips back to Illinois from Texas, we took a detour into Memphis, Tennessee and then on to Graceland. We couldn't afford the tour of Elvis Presley's mansion, but I took a lot of pictures of Lexi in front of the gates and the airplane. I bought her an Elvis Presley Coca Cola, too. Then I said, "Hey, your uncles have never been to Mississippi," and off we went to Mississippi, which was only about five miles away, to take a picture of Lexi there. She made sure her uncles found out about it later, of course.

We didn't have a lot, but we made the most of what we had, like visiting the world's biggest candy store. We just tried to have a little fun and see the sights whenever we could. If it was something that her uncles hadn't done, she was all for it because then she could tell them, "I did it. You didn't."

Lexi, Uncle Wes, Uncle Thomas

By the time Lexi turned five, it was time for kindergarten, and I was in a panic. I didn't think I'd properly prepared Lexi for it. My granddad had been a math teacher, a principal, and a school superintendent. He used to play games with us. We didn't realize that it was actually educational. We thought it was just fun and games, but I was reading and doing math at an early age. He actually had me reading the Bible and the Los Angeles Times by the age of two.

When I met her kindergarten teacher and principal for the first time, I started crying and apologizing for not teaching Lexi how to read already. The teacher just looked at me and said, "Uh, they're in kindergarten. None of them can read more than a couple of words here and there." I said, "No, every good parent has their children reading at age two." She just looked at me quizzically, and I could tell in her mind she was saying said, "What is wrong with you?"

That teacher was right. Lexi was just fine, and she soon became a voracious reader. She loved reading, especially the Harry Potter book series.

CHAPTER 2
OUT OF RIGHT FIELD

*"All of life is peaks and valleys. Don't let the peaks
get too high and the valleys too low."*
– JOHN WOODEN

By the spring of '98, we'd lived up in Illinois for almost four years by ourselves. It was just the two of us, but that was about to change. Twice.

Some people who I met at a gym were putting together a co-rec softball team, needed more girls, and invited me to play. I was a nerd, not an athlete, but I agreed to stand out there if they needed another female.

One day, I was playing right field and went for a fly ball to my right. The guy in right-center field went for it too, and we literally ran into each other trying to catch it. As it turned out, I missed the ball—we both did—but I caught the guy. His name was Chris Conerty.

We met to play darts later that week. I wasn't interested when he told me that he was a banker, but then he mentioned that he did some farming. That was different, in a good way. I couldn't care less about the rich corporate types, but I grew up on a ranch in a rural area and loved to talk about those times. We hit it off and started dating.

Lexi turned nine that November, and she wasn't the sole focus of my attention anymore. There was someone else, and some friction in our mother-daughter relationship developed for the first time. I wasn't worried about it at the time, but I understand in hindsight why she didn't like it. I went out on dates occasionally before Chris, but I'd never been that serious with anyone before. It was just Lexi and me for eight and a half years.

Chris and I married in March of '99 in a small wedding service in Texas. I was a 32-year old doctoral student on spring break. Lexi was my bridesmaid. She looked beautiful, played a role in the wedding, and things got a little bit better afterwards, but she still seemed to resent that she didn't have my sole attention anymore. This was new, but not improved, at least not for her.

There were more big changes in store as well. We moved to Urbana, Illinois, and Lexi had to change schools in the fourth grade. By that time, kids have their little cliques, and Lexi was leaving behind so many friends from kindergarten, first, second, and third grade. We didn't move that far geographically, but it was a huge adjustment for a young girl, and I didn't realize how it was affecting Lexi.

She started acting out a little more. She was more withdrawn than usual and not as happy as she'd been all of her life. Part of it could have been attributable to the fact that she was pre-teen. Adolescents often want to assert their independence, but there was clearly something else going on.

By this time, I was tired of my doctoral program in finance. I just couldn't conduct research for the rest of my life and started looking for something else. Later that year, a teaching opportunity arose at Parkland College, a two-year community college across town from the University of Illinois, and I decided to give it a try. To my surprise and slight embarrassment, I really enjoyed it. Like so many others in my family, I liked to teach.

My new teaching job also freed up time in my schedule to hang out with Lexi and attend more of her school functions. It was great, but before I knew it, terrorists were flying airplanes into buildings on September 11, 2001, and I panicked. I was teaching that day and couldn't wait to pick her up from school. I stayed there during her school cheerleading practice, and I hugged her more than usual. It was a horrible day for the country, but it brought Lexi and me a little closer again.

Lexi's relationship with my new husband and her new stepdad Chris was unpredictable and occasionally intense. They were cool at first and had fun together at times, but then it would take a sudden turn for the worse. It reminded me of the relationship with my stepdad when I was her age. It took me a few years to accept him after my mother remarried. I didn't even acknowledge his existence for a few years, and I lashed out at my mom. Later on, he became my dad, and I can't imagine my life without him.

In some ways, I can understand why Lexi had so much trouble accepting Chris. My natural father left my mother, my siblings and me, but at least I knew and remembered him before a stepdad joined the family. Lexi never had a dad before. She had good male role models in my stepdad and granddad, as well as in her uncles and other family members, but she'd never known her natural father. Now a new guy was trying to play the part.

Chris is a good and patient man, and he tried to make it work with Lexi. He'd been married before, but he didn't have any kids or experience in something like this. He was trying to live under the same roof with two other highly independent people who knew each other very well already.

Chris came out of right field—well, center-right field—and he didn't come alone. I got pregnant again. I was 36, Lexi was 14, and now there was going to be another person in the house who needed my attention.

I thought Lexi might be upset about the prospect of another child in the house, and she did say things like "Seriously!" and "You're too old" at times during the pregnancy, but she adored her baby sister from the start and couldn't wait to meet her. Unbeknownst to me, she gushed about it to her teachers, friends, and acquaintances. "I'm going to have a little sister! I'm going to be a big sister! I can't wait," she'd exclaim. There was a 14-year age difference, but she didn't care. She beamed and couldn't wait to teach her baby sister how to play volleyball and basketball, and how to sing in the choir.

Lexi and her new little sister, Stasia

My second little girl, Anastasia (or "Stasia"), was born on October 27, 2003, and she was big! Stasia was a big, cheerful, healthy baby, and Lexi was adapting perfectly, but then something unexpected and horrible hit us out of *left* field: Postpartum depression.

I didn't know what was wrong with me, and I was too stubborn to seek treatment for feeling blue, but I should have and wish I did. It was more than just the baby blues. It was horrible, and it wreaked havoc on all of my relationships. Severe depression, like teaching, ran in my family, but I'd never struggled with it like this until after Stasia was born. I'm not sure how much of it had to do with my advanced age because it didn't happen after Lexi was born, but my hormones were completely out of whack and stayed that way for two years.

I got on Lexi for so many things. It was a whirlwind, with yelling and horrible things said on both parts. There were even a few physical tussles, but nothing serious. I remember her screaming "I hate you!" and saying that she wished she'd never been born, wished she had a different father, mother, or whatever, and things like that but—in her defense—I really wasn't a nice person back then. I snapped at everybody, didn't care about their reaction, and this went on day after day.

One day, she got so angry at me that she told the school resource officer, "I don't want to go home," and they intervened. A police officer called me to say that Lexi was scared, and someone from the Department of Children and Family Services wanted to have a talk with me. Well, we talked about it, and I began to realize that something might be wrong with me. It's hard for me to admit and remember, but it happened.

We found out later that I was suffering from severe, untreated depression. We also learned, as you'll see in the next Chapter, that Lexi had a physical problem of her own. These chemical and physical imbalances fueled outbursts from both of us during that difficult period, but we didn't know it at the time. We were just a mother and daughter going at each other all the time for one reason or another.

In hindsight, I regret every horrible thing I ever said to Lexi, Chris (who bore the brunt of much of it), Stasia, and others during those two years, and it's been hard living with the guilt since Lexi passed away.

Changes came out of right field and left for Lexi during these years but, to her credit, she never stopped enjoying her life and pursuing her dreams. She somehow managed to find herself in middle school and was exceptionally comfortable in her own skin after that. She met more people, made friends everywhere she went, and stayed active. Things were tense at home, but still had a ball playing with her baby sister – I have so many pictures with Lexi lovingly holding Stasia – and she was still the same active, affable, highly sociable teenager every place else she went.

Lexi and Stasia

Lexi and Stasia

Lexi and Stasia

Lexi and Stasia

Lexi, Stasia, and Mimi

Lexi at 4-H Summer Camp

Lexi

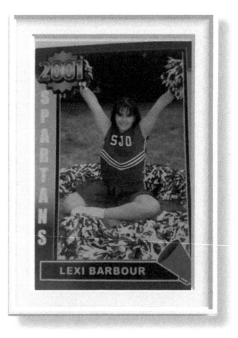

*Lexi, St. Joseph Middle
School Basketball*

*Lexi, St. Joseph Youth
Cheerleading*

Lexi enjoyed many sports and athletic activities, including basketball, volleyball, ice skating, roller skating, and watching football. She was an average athlete, but she was happy just to be part of the team. It didn't matter if she was riding the bench. She'd cheer just as loudly as anybody else.

But there was one sport that Lexi loved most of all, cheerleading. She participated in youth cheerleading in the 4th, 5th, 6th, 7th and 8th grades and cheered with the other girls at youth football games every Sunday afternoon. Close friendships developed at different schools in the area, which made Lexi's transition to a new school much smoother. She was always part of the cheerleading base, where they would lift other girls up and things like that. It wasn't easy. It was a real sport in many ways.

Naturally, after so many years of youth cheerleading, Lexi dreamed of becoming a high school varsity cheerleader, and making the squad at St. Joseph / Ogden High School in St. Joseph, Illinois became one of her major goals in life. They held the tryouts for the high school team at the middle school when she was in 8th grade, and she was so excited about cheering in her freshman year. She practiced at home— in the backyard, front yard, living room, bedroom, kitchen, shower, and everywhere else—went to the audition, and didn't make the cut.

She was devastated. It killed me to see her crying because she'd been so enthusiastic and optimistic about the opportunity. I did my best to comfort her, and she initiated a hug with me for one of the few times in her teenage years. We talked about it through the tears, and she resolved to keep practicing and try again the following year. I said, "If this is something you really want to do, we'll do whatever you need to do. Not everything works out right the first time."

She kept improving by practicing on her own and working with some of her friends who were already on the cheer squad and willing to help. She didn't let disappointment keep her from going to the games and sitting in the student cheering section with her other friends, either. It was never all about her. She was always a team player.

In the spring of her freshman year, she practiced her cheers even harder and tried out again to become a member of the varsity squad as a sophomore, but the result was the same. She didn't make the cut. She was so confident that she was going to make it after another year of practice and hard work, but she failed again, and it hurt just as much, if not more.

Most kids would have thrown in the towel on their dream and move on to something else after failing twice. It hurts, and it's embarrassing. Not Lexi. Another year passed and there she was, trying out in the spring of her sophomore year to become a member of the varsity cheerleading squad as a junior. Only this time, she made it! I swear her feet didn't touch the ground for the rest of the day. She was on Cloud 9, giggling and squealing, with the biggest grin ever plastered on her face.

After that, for days on end, all she talked about was cheer camp. She was always on the phone with her friends, excitedly making plans to get cheerleading shoes—the shoes were a very big deal—matching T-shirts, scrunchies, and other stuff for camp. She had persevered and made her dream come true at last; she was high school varsity cheerleader, and she was thrilled.

When Lexi wasn't cheering, she was singing beautifully, or so it seemed. She played the clarinet in her 5th and 6th grade band and liked it, but she liked singing more and followed her passion for it into the high school choir. They had the spring, fall, and winter concerts, and then regional and stage contests, and she was always in there. She sang in her room, the car, and the shower, too, and she occasionally talked about possibly following in the footsteps of my cousin, Laura Sullivan, who's a Grammy award-winning professional musician.

Lexi loved to sing acapella with her friends at church, as well. The church youth group had all sorts of fun Sunday-School type activities, like playing miniature gold, going for ice cream, and going to the movies, but Lexi enjoyed the youth group meetings on Wednesday nights the most and made sure to show up to meet her friends there every week. The youth minister would teach them about morality, spirituality, and religion without all the hell fire and brimstone or adults standing there shaking their heads, or a finger. They usually met away from the church building itself so the kids could relax and learn things while they were having fun.

Lexi and Philo Road church of Christ youth group

I don't know if Lexi was "religious" in a traditional sense, but she was spiritual, and you could hear it in the angelic way she sang. And every once in a while, she would sit and calmly look outside at the trees or the flowers. She'd do that to center herself, contemplate things, or meditate in her own way. Then, she'd go back to being a crazy teenager.

I grew up going to church every weekend and kept going when Lexi and Stasia were young, but I don't know that I was so religious. I think I just enjoyed socializing with a lot of good people. So did Lexi. I didn't have to twist her arm to join me on Sundays, either. She wanted to go with me, and that's what we did for about five years. Then, she'd be back there again every Wednesday night for the youth ministry.

Of course, young teenage girls also start getting crushes on boys, and Lexi was no different. She seemed to take an interest in a different boy every other week and went on a few dates, but nothing serious ever came of it until she was about 15. One day, while I was driving Lexi to the public swimming pool in Champaign, she was like, "Yeah mom, by the way, I want you to meet somebody." When I pulled up, a nice looking young man was waiting to meet her, and she was like, "Yeah, this is Ryan, my boyfriend." I was like, "Okay."

Ryan brought Lexi to his homecoming, prom, and everything else, and their boyfriend-girlfriend relationship continued literally until the day she died. He was Lexi's first love and, as it turns out, the only love of her life.

Lexi and Ryan, Centennial High
School Homecoming, 2004

Lexi was a happy go-lucky teenager, even when my postpartum depression made it difficult to stay that way at home. She didn't need to be the most popular kid at school, and she didn't need to be the star of the cheerleading squad, church group, volleyball team, choir, school play, or any other team, group, or club she joined. She was happy just to be there. To this day, her friends tell me how Lexi would always crack everybody up. She was a class clown without being goofy or rebellious.

I wasn't like Lexi as a teenager. I studied constantly, always had my nose in a book, and didn't get involved in many extracurricular activities. But we loved each other and shared many common interests, including Stasia, athletics, church activities, reading—she adored the Harry Potter books—and watching silly, stupid movies. I actually got her hooked on the Monty Python movies. We'd sit and watch them together, and I was so proud that the humor didn't go over her head. It takes a special kind of personality to really "get" that brand of comedy, and she certainly did.

I baked a homemade banana nut cake on my 39th birthday and, as was our custom for at least ten years, Lexi handled the frosting. This time, she made cream cheese frosting and got it all over the thing. Then she wrote "Happy 39th Birthday, Kelly" with a tube of icing gel on the top, placed candles in a 3 and 9 pattern because she couldn't fit 39 candles on there, and lit them. It was a special day, and we continued growing closer again as mother and daughter in the next few months, but there was trouble ahead—lots of it—and I never saw it coming.

CHAPTER 3

A BLOOD CLOT NAMED ED

"It was the best of times, it was the worst of times."
– CHARLES DICKENS, *A TALE OF TWO CITIES*

Lexi had recently achieved a multi-year dream: She made the varsity high school cheerleading squad after three years of trying out. She liked school mainly because it was a great place to socialize with her friends, and there was no better way to do that then become a varsity cheerleader, and she couldn't have been more excited about it.

The weather was warming up in the middle of May, towards the end of the school year, and she was busy excitedly making plans for cheerleader camp with other girls on the squad. They needed matching shirts, scrunchies, and the whole nine yards.

Lexi was 16 now. She had a driver's license, a job at the local roller skating rink, and tons of friends to go out with, but she was tired of school and ready for summer vacation.

Over the last few months, Lexi's right arm had been getting sore and swelling up a little bit. So we took her to the convenient care center a few times to have it examined. The doctors reassured us that it wasn't broken, thought it was probably just a little sprain, and recommended that we treat it with some old-fashioned ice and ibuprofen. We followed doctors' orders, but it got worse, and it was tough for Lexi to do many things because she was right-handed, like me.

Everything changed on Tuesday, May 23, 2006, the beginning of five weeks of hell. It was a warm day, but Lexi's arm was really swollen and ice cold. This time, Chris took Lexi to our primary care physician, Dr. Lee, half-expecting to hear that there was a strain, minor hairline fracture, or something like that. Instead, she immediately sent them to the cardiology wing of the local hospital, where I met Chris and Lexi. Dr. Lee's husband worked as a cardiologist, and she knew right away it was serious. After a few tests, they broke the news. Lexi had a blot clot. They told us to go home and bring her a bag with her things because she wasn't going home for a while.

I was astonished. You hear all of these stories on TV about people getting blood clots and dying after long plane trips or whatever, but Lexi hadn't done anything like that. They said, in essence, "Nope. She's staying. We're admitting her. We're going to start her on blood thinners immediately, and we're going to schedule surgery tomorrow morning." There was no time to wait because the blood clot was located just under her collar bone. If it moved, it would travel directly to the brain and kill her.

That was all I needed to hear. After driving home to pick up Lexi's things, I returned to the hospital and stayed in the ICU waiting room while Lexi was being pumped full of blood thinners. The waiting room was full of people in their seventies and eighties. I was terrified but tried to smile and pretend I wasn't because Lexi didn't appear overly concerned. When the nurses had her set up in a room, Lexi was kidding around and calling her friends to reassure them that she was fine and to catch up on everything else that was happening.

It was the first time in my life that I felt completely helpless and lost. I had zero control over this. In the past, when Lexi came home with bumps and bruises, I could handle it. Moms can always put a band aid on a minor injury, kiss, and fix it, but I couldn't fix a blood clot. I didn't know what to do or how to deal with it other than to let the doctors do their thing and hope for the best.

Coincidentally, the very same morning of the same day that they first discovered Lexi's blood clot, I had an appointment with a physician to address my postpartum depression and started on anti-depressants. The drugs certainly helped, but they didn't snap me out of my depression. The blood clot did. I was so laser focused on regaining control of Lexi's situation and my life that I didn't have the luxury of thinking or worrying about anything else. I spent all of my time talking to doctors, doing research, trying to remain upbeat and optimistic, and living at the hospital with Lexi. Everything else was of secondary importance and could take care of itself.

That first night, I watched as my baby girl finally fell asleep hooked up to IV's and needles and everything else and surrounded by all sorts of machines. Other than the occasional common cold or ear infection, she'd been healthy her entire life, like most people in my family, who almost always live long lives. And, except for all of the medical equipment around her, Lexi still looked normal lying there on the hospital bed, but I knew the truth. She had a life-threatening condition that could have killed her instantly, and she was still in danger without emergency care and surgery.

The next day, the time for Lexi's surgery arrived. The nurses could tell that I was going a little crazy and told me to go home… go somewhere, but get out of the hospital. It was going to be a 3-hour surgery, and there was nothing I could do to help in the meantime. I didn't want to stray too far from the hospital, however, in case they finished early or something went wrong. So, I just drove around. I kept thinking how Lexi should be at a cheerleader meeting, hanging out with friends, at work, or chatting on the phone, not about to be cut open.

In hindsight, I was clearly in no condition to be driving around aimlessly and shouldn't have done so. It's a big mistake to drive when you're not clear-headed and focused, but I found myself at a red light in Campus Town, over by the University of Illinois. I looked to my left, noticed a parlor offering tattoos and piercings, and pulled up in front.

I entered, told them what was happening, heard about their services, and said, "Why not? Let's get my belly button pierced." People always say that acupuncture and things like that are very cathartic, and that's what happened in my case. It was only a little painful, but it calmed me down, like a slap of cold water to the face snaps a hysterical person out of it in the movies. I started breathing and regained my focus. I emerged from the fog and returned to the hospital, less of a basket case.

Lexi had been asking for a piercing of her own for a while, but I wouldn't allow it because she wasn't old enough, even after she called me old and boring. So, imagine her surprise when she woke up after her surgery and I lifted my shirt a little to show her something. She squealed in delight and yelled for the nurses. When they rushed in to find out what was wrong, Lexi said her mother was "crazy" and "the coolest person in the world." Then she insisted that I show them my new belly button piercing.

One by one, the nurses came into Lexi's room to show us the piercings and tattoos they got on a "margarita night" a few months earlier. It was hilarious. Everyone was telling stories, laughing, and having fun. And, for the first time since she was two or three years old, Lexi thought I was really cool.

When the laughter subsided, the nurses explained that it was going to take a little while for Lexi to fully recover. The doctor had successfully dissolved the blood clot during surgery, but they had to keep Lexi in the hospital for a while on heavy blood thinners to ensure that the clot didn't return and to minimize the risk of additional clotting.

A day or two later, one of Lexi's friends from the cheerleading squad called to tell her that their matching shoes had arrived. She was thrilled and immediately turned to me and said, ""Mother, go get my shoes. Do not come back to this hospital without them." The rest of her uniform hadn't arrived, but it didn't matter. She had been gleefully planning for cheer camp with her friends non-stop. A silly blood clot wasn't going to interfere with that, and she wanted those shoes most of all.

When I retrieved the beautiful white cheer shoes and gave them to her for the first time, she could not have been happier. She would often just admire them, get dreamy eyed, and smile. You could see the movie of her future cheering on the sidelines of the football field playing in her head. Sometimes, she'd dust and polish them too, but she never tried the shoes on because she didn't need to, at least not yet. They already served as tangible proof that she had persevered and overcome two heartbreaking failures to make the team; she made a dream come true and achieved a major goal in life.

Lexi remained in the ICU for a week after her initial surgery to dissolve the clot. Everything looked good, and they began to ween her off of the blood thinners for a couple of days, but the doctor noticed something during Lexi's surgery that caused some concern. One of her top ribs had been rubbing up against the vein and created scar tissue that was putting pressure on it. They weren't sure, but they thought this might explain how the blood clot formed and wanted to address the problem at its source. So, on Tuesday morning of the following week (Monday was Memorial Day), they performed another surgery to remove the top rib and clean up the scar tissue. When it was over, Lexi needed another four more days to recover.

By the time Lexi finally left the hospital, she'd been there almost two full weeks. They told us that the surgery was successful and should prevent a reoccurrence, which was great news. So, as soon as we got home, Lexi was on the phone, and her friends were coming over to celebrate. She wasn't quite ready to drive anywhere yet since the pain medication was still wearing off and her right shoulder was sore from surgery. I drove Lexi and her friends to the mall, where they hung out and goofed around like always. Many of her friends visited Lexi in the hospital, but she had missed seeing them on a daily basis.

Things were better than ever. After about three years of mother-teenage daughter angst and severe postpartum depression, it was gone in a flash. It was wonderful, and I thought we'd really dodged a bullet as a family. We'd survived the worst thing that could ever happen to a young, healthy teenager and emerged with our priorities better aligned and a renewed love and appreciation for each other. Life was great, and we'd never have to worry about anything like that again.

Not so fast.

Lexi had only been home for a week when I received a call from the mother of one of her friends while I was working out at the gym. They were at the emergency room because Lexi's arm went numb and cold again. I freaked out, sped to the hospital, rushed to the triage room, and found Lexi there laughing it up with a couple friends as if nothing was wrong even though they had her hooked up to things and nurses were busily coming and going. I'm thinking, how did she get another blood clot when she was on blood thinners? How did this happen if the surgery was a success?

When I walked up to the hospital bed to see how she was doing, Lexi said, "Yeah, Ed's back." I said, "What? Who's Ed?" Ed was the name of her blood clot. Yep, as it turns out, Lexi and her friends had previously given her blot clot a name, Ed, and he was back. They called it Ed based on an episode of a series on the Cartoon Network where one of the three Ed's—Ed, Edd, and Eddy—had a bump or something, and everybody was making fun of him. Lexi may have been hooked up with wires and tubes again, but she had the nurses, a doctor, and friends cracking up every time she mentioned "Ed."

At one point, after she'd been on blood thinners for a while, they tried to put another IV into Lexi's arm and apparently missed the mark. Blood spurted all over the place because it was so thin, but Lexi wasn't worried in the least. She just kept joking around.

This time, the doctor and nurses told us that, if they weren't able to dissolve the clot with the blood thinners and other less intrusive means, they may need to do a fairly routine bypass of the vein with the blot clot because so much scar tissue had built up where the rib had been rubbing against it since she was a little girl. We had plans to take a trip to St. Louis, but that could wait. Ed was back, and he had to go.

Over the next few days, while Lexi was on blood thinners, I spent most of my time at the hospital. Fortunately, I didn't have to go to the college to work because all of the classes that I taught during the summer were online. So, I could spend all of my time with Lexi or driving all over the county picking up friends and hauling them to the hospital, or running other errands like renting movies at Blockbuster to watch on the VCR that nurses had kindly hooked up in Lexi's room. I got some really stupid, silly movies, including *Super Troopers,* which we watched together at least four times.

While I cared for Lexi and kept her company, my husband Chris (who worked as a farmer on the farm that surrounded our house), his parents, and my dad watched Stasia, who was barely two and a half years old. My dad, a kind, quiet, thoughtful and loving man, had driven up to Illinois for a few weeks, as he did from time to time, to see the kids and help around the farm. He used to enjoy going to Lexi's volleyball games, Stasia's preschool plays, and things like that. He also spent some time at the hospital with Lexi and me, of course. Nobody else in my family came up.

They let Stasia visit her big sister a few times as well, and she loved it. The nurses would bring her popsicles, and Stasia loved to play with the balloons that others had brought for Lexi. She also liked to hold Lexi on her good side, and sometimes Lexi would make the bed go up and down with Stasia beside her. Stasia would giggle every time it happened. Then Lexi would start giggling, and pretty soon the nurses and I were laughing too. It was so cute.

Many others came to visit Lexi during her three weeks in the hospital with a blood clot named Ed, including so many of her good friends, but she and I had a chance spent a lot of quality time together during that period because it was usually just the two of us, like old times. If she was in the hospital, so was I.

Fortunately, after another week in the ICU, Ed was gone… again. They discharged Lexi from the hospital once again, and she came home. We had dodged another bullet, but we were still going to look into travelling to St. Louis for the vein bypass surgery. We didn't want this to keep happening.

The good times continued for the next week because Lexi and I were close again. She was super-excited about cheerleading camp, and I was just so glad that she was home, alive and well. I didn't want to sweat the small stuff anymore—like giving her a hard time if she pulled a "C" on a test—and I certainly wasn't going to do it to Stasia.

In hindsight, oh my gosh, I am so grateful for those five special weeks as mother and daughter with Lexi. Our relationship had suffered under the weight of my postpartum depression and the regular stress and strain of life for a few years, but for those five weeks, she thought I was cool. She wanted me to brush her hair. She wanted me to hold her. She wanted to watch silly movies with me and laugh together. She wanted me to be there. We loved each other and bonded again.

I also started to appreciate Lexi more for just who she was (not who I wanted to mold her to be), and her incredible talent, spirit, and personality. I started paying attention to how she laughed when her friends came to the hospital and how she talked with them in person and over the phone. And it carried over to how I viewed my other lovable baby girl, Stasia. I began to look at both of them differently, rethink my priorities, pick my battles, and count my blessings. I already had too many regrets, and I didn't want to spend another moment of their lives or mine preoccupied with insignificant things.

So, as bad as it was dealing with blood clots and nights at the hospital, those five weeks were awesome for bringing us together as a family. But that's not the only reason I cherish them. As it turns out, it was all the time Lexi and I would ever have together.

I know that many grieving parents don't get weeks or even days to set things right before their children die, like I did. If that includes you, God bless you. We never know when it's going to happen. I certainly didn't, and Lexi could easily have died sooner.

Each of us has a story about the relationship with our child before they died, and it can get complicated, especially during the teenage years. We endure what we think is the worst that can happen to them—an arrest, drug use, injury, poor grades, or something like that, and teenagers are often pretty messed up physiologically, psychologically, or chemically. They're trying to find themselves and grow through a typically awkward stage of life, and it can be hard for even the most loving of parents to deal with it.

But we can't blow things out of proportion. Too often, it's only after a child dies that grieving parents realize that all of those events that we thought were the worst thing that could ever happen to our child really weren't such a big deal after all.

There is something worse, much worse: Initiation into the Grieving Parents Club.

CHAPTER 4

JOINING THE CLUB

A single twig breaks, but the bundle of twigs is strong."

- TECUMSEH

June 28, 2006: "There Was Nothing We Could Do"

It was a warm, beautiful, early summer day on Wednesday, June 28, 2006 in Urbana, Illinois. Lexi had been home for about a week after her second stay in the hospital. She was inside the house because I'd asked her to watch Stasia, who was just 2 and ½ years old at the time, while I worked outside in the garden and enjoyed the sunshine.

When I came back into the house, I saw them lying on the bed together watching SpongeBob SquarePants on TV and giggling. Then Lexi got up, brought me her most recent paycheck from her job at the skating rink, and asked me if I would cash it for her because she was running late. It was about 6:55pm, and she was supposed to meet with other members of her youth group at 7:00pm at the church, which was only about 5 minutes away by car. After I agreed to do it, Lexi gave Stasia a little tickle, quickly hugged me and said, "Bye mom. Love you. See you later." Then she got into the car, pulled out of the driveway, and drove off toward the church.

About 30 minutes later, around 7:25pm—these times and dates are ingrained in my memory forever—a sheriff's deputy came kind of racing down the road and pulled into our driveway. Chris and I were friends with a lot of the deputies, so it wasn't unusual for them to stop by, but no one had ever raced down the road into the drive. When he told me that Lexi had been in an accident and airlifted to the hospital, I remember thinking that I needed to get to the hospital to give them my insurance card and be with Lexi, but I never once thought it was serious because bad stuff just didn't happen in my family. I was worried, of course, but airlifting her to a hospital located just 5 miles away seemed like overkill. It didn't make any sense to me. I assumed that there'd be bumps and bruises, or maybe a broken bone or concussion, but that's it.

I didn't speed to the hospital because I still thought everything was going to be fine. I parked my car, walked calmly into the emergency room, and told the lady at the registration desk that my daughter had been brought in. I was ready to hand over the insurance cards and sign forms authorizing treatment, but that's when it got weird. She looked something up on the computer, got very quiet, and said "Just a moment."

While I was waiting and looking around in the ER lobby, somebody in a white coat came toward me and said, "Come on back." She avoided eye contact with me as she walked me into the operating room, where I saw Lexi's body lying on a cold, stainless steel table, with doctors and nurses in white coats standing around her. People were yelling, screaming, grabbing medical utensils, and moving stuff back and forth. All I could see were legs and feet, but I knew it was Lexi. I thought, "No. This isn't real. She's only 16. She's supposed to be at church. Why isn't she at church? Why is she lying on that table?"

Finally, I said something like, "Please, help her. That's my daughter." Someone barked "Get out" and another person escorted me out of the OR and into a small room adjacent to the larger waiting room. Chris met me there, and we weren't there for long before a doctor and a nurse walked in to deliver the news. With their heads bowed and eyes lowered—they wouldn't look us in the eyes—they said, "We're sorry. There was nothing we could do. Your daughter is dead."

It didn't register. I thought, "Sorry? Sorry for what? Nothing we could do? What does that mean?" An hour or two ago, my two baby girls were watching cartoons and having fun. Now, they're telling me that Lexi is dead? This was not happening to me. It couldn't possibly be true. This kind of thing doesn't happen in my family. It must be a nightmare or a sick joke. I wanted someone to wake me up, throw cold water on me, slap my face, or snap me out of it in some other way, but nobody did, and there I was.

I went into a daze or trance, where everything around me moved in slow motion. Voices and other sounds were muted. It was like a dream sequence that we've all seen on TV or at the movies, but this time I wasn't watching the action from a safe distance as part of the audience. I was right in the middle of it, and I didn't know what to say, do, or feel.

My life had changed in the blink of an eye, and I didn't have time to prepare or steel myself for it. I was wrong about the blood-clot scare being the worst thing that could happen to a healthy, happy-go-lucky teenager like Lexi. Things could and did get much worse. She died suddenly at the age of 16, and I would never be the same. They offer classes to help you prepare for the birth of a child, but not for the death of a child, even though the pain and sense of loss is unlike and arguably worse than any other.

I didn't realize it yet, but I had joined a club for parents who bury their children. A wife becomes a "widow" when her husband dies, and a child becomes an "orphan" when his parents pass away, but what does a parent become when their child dies before they do? There really isn't a good name for it because it's never supposed to happen and no one wants to think about it. But parents who bury their children are forever bound together in something that I call the "Grieving Parents Club" or simply the "Club."

Admission to the Club is automatic, involuntary, and unnatural. Nobody wants to join, and everybody would give anything to get out, but it doesn't work that way. We are initiated into the Club the moment our child dies, whether from an accident, illness and disease, suicide, homicide, or any other way, and we remain a member until the day we, too, die. Sometimes, it reminds me of the old Eagles song, *Hotel California*, because you can check out anytime you like, but you can never leave.

The Grieving Parents Club may be grounded in tragedy and pain but, as I would soon discover, there's something special, even invaluable, about it, too. It's filled with some of the kindest, most caring people you will ever meet or know. All they want to do is welcome, help and guide other grieving parents through the difficult days to come, and they do it in a way that no one else can.

Other members of the Club were the only ones who could possibly have understood and empathized with the pain I felt in the hospital upon learning of Lexi's death, but they weren't around, and I didn't even know how much I needed them. I felt lost, alone, and utterly disoriented. It was a dark and scary place, a place that I would visit many times in the years to come. The emotional and physical pain was excruciating and, like other new members of the Club, I wasn't sure if I could live with it.

It's Not Okay

I had to get out of the hospital and get some fresh air. I was suffocating and couldn't bear to watch the surreal scene inside anymore, but reality still hadn't sunk in. Chris and I somehow found ourselves walking outside the emergency room area and over to a little park across the street from the hospital where I slowly paced back and forth down the sidewalk. As I paced, it dawned on me that I should tell my family what was happening. I didn't know if I could reach my mother or sisters because they often went to a church service on Wednesday nights, but I lifted my cellphone, dialed my sister's number, and watched myself do it like I was having an of out-of-body experience.

My sister answered, and I was a little surprised that she did. Then, in a very calm, almost monotone voice, I told her that Lexi was in an accident, and she didn't make it. After she reacted, I asked her to please tell everyone else, and I hung up. Now, I really felt like I was going to faint. So, I slowly walked over to a grassy area just outside the ER and sat down.

People started showing up within minutes. Soon there was a circle of people all around me, sobbing and looking down at me with pity, and I hated it. Some came straight from church, including the youth minister and members of Lexi's youth group, and they were praying as they cried. Not me. I still wasn't really crying, and I didn't want to pray. I was still in shock and waiting for the dream to end.

A few people tried to sit next to me or put their arm around me, but no one really managed to comfort or affect me in any way until Lexi's boyfriend, Ryan, came over and sat down. I could see how distraught he was and thought, "Oh, my gosh. I've got to play mom." I put my arm around him, held him, and patted him on the back while he sobbed. I said, "It's okay" to make him feel better, but then he started to cry, and that was it. I lost it. It finally hit me: Lexi was dead, and it wasn't okay.

People stuck around for hours, and it got late. Then, around 9 or 9:30 pm, somebody walked out of the hospital, looked for me, and asked if I wanted to see Lexi once more before the coroner took her away. I'd been very calm all night, but I couldn't take it anymore. I yelled, "No. I don't want to see her zipped up in a bag!" I had already seen her naked body on the stainless steel table in the operating room. I didn't want to see any more. I was just screaming "No, no, no! I don't want to see her like that. I don't want to see her zipped up in a bag." Chris went to see her, but I couldn't do it.

A friend drove me home at about 11pm. People came over and stayed for hours, but I just sat on the wicker patio furniture on my front porch, just staring silently into the darkness across miles. My memories of Lexi were still so fresh—she had hugged me just a little over 4 hours ago!—and now she wasn't coming home again. Ever. At about 3am, I finally went into the house, lay down on the bed, and stared at the ceiling. It would become the first of many sleepless nights over the next few years.

The next thing I knew, it was morning. There were still all sorts of people in and around the house and cars all over the place, but I wasn't interested in talking to anyone. I walked out to my garden, plopped down in the dirt, and started pulling weeds by hand. I needed to do something, stay busy, get my hands dirty, and take my fury and frustration out on the weeds.

I'd been sitting cross-legged in the dirt, yelling at weeds for about an hour when my parents arrived at the house after taking a late-night flight from Dallas / Ft. Worth, Texas. My mom was sobbing and told me my brothers and sisters were on the way up by car. At first, all I could think was, "Oh, I can't handle this right now." So, I kept digging in the dirt, but then I thought, "Well, there are enough people here now. Maybe I should go play hostess. Can I get anybody something to eat?" By now, car after car was starting to show up with food, and I had to make sure that everybody had enough to eat and drink, or so I thought. I wasn't punishing weeds anymore. I'd calmed down a little bit, but I was still in a surreal daze.

At around 5pm, I started to panic and become almost paranoid about something happening to Stasia, too. We had taken her to preschool in the morning to keep her life on schedule, but it was almost 5pm. So, I wondered, "Is she okay? Did somebody go pick her up? Somebody needs to pick her up!" I said it repeatedly, and I was extremely anxious until she returned home and I could hug her. Then she went off to play as if nothing were wrong, and she was having a ball. She had all kinds of people to play with who brought her toys, flowers, food, and stuffed animals, and she was too young to know about or understand what had happened to her big sister yesterday.

After a while, the noise, crying, pitiful eyes, and unsolicited advice about how I should speak to a counselor or minister right away, were too much to bear. I had to get out of the house. It was Thursday afternoon, not quite 24 hours since Lexi died. I grabbed my phone and went for a walk toward the corn fields. I needed to talk with somebody about Lexi's death, but I wasn't looking for platitudes, prayers, pity, or "professional" advice. I needed to speak with someone who could truly empathize with my situation and potentially say or do something helpful. In other words, I needed to reach out to other members of the Club who knew me and Lexi well, and that's what I did.

Turning to Other Club Members for the First Time

The first person I called was a relatively new member of the Club, Elgin Lary. He knew Lexi well because we had attended college together in Texas and had been friends for years. His teenaged son, James Lee, had died in a drunk-driving accident only three months earlier, and I knew how hard he was taking it. I also knew that he had joined "Compassionate Friends," a national organization with small support groups here and there for people who've lost children or grandchildren, and I wondered if I should too.

Elgin responded much differently to news of Lexi's death than anyone else had so far. He was like, "I know how it is. Are you sleeping? Has it sunk in yet?" He said, "It took a long time for me to recover. I was in this dream-daze state." When I said, "No, I'm kind of in a daze right now," he added, "Well, you're going to have to make some decisions pretty soon, and you're going to have moments when you'll come out of that daze." He was able to prepare me for what was coming because he had just recently lived through it. He basically said, "Okay, in the next couple of days, this is what's going to happen."

Then I called a long-term member of the Club whom I'd known for decades, Mrs. Maxine Stillwell. Her younger daughter had died of leukemia 20 or 30 years ago, and her older daughter was killed by a drunk driver. She was a breast cancer survivor, too. She was a sweet Southern woman, but she was tough as nails. She'd been through it all and was still out there smiling. I had to know how she did it.

I told Mrs. Stillwell what had happened and how I didn't know what to do. I asked her questions like, "How do you keep going? You've lost two daughters, and then you had to deal with breast cancer. How do you get up in the morning? How do you still smile? How are you so cheerful? And how can I get through this?" Then she gave me the best advice. She said, "Sugar, don't you give a *damn* what those Yankees think. You're the mama. You be selfish for once in your life. When you want to talk, you talk. When you're done talking, you're done talking."

First of all, I thought, "Oh my goodness, Mrs. Stillwell just said 'damn,'" and I laughed out loud for the first time since Lexi died. She was a good Southern Baptist woman whom I had known since I was 15 years old. I had never heard her cuss before, but she just did it that day to make sure I got the message when I needed it most. Moms aren't supposed to be selfish. We're supposed to take care of everyone else's needs before our own, but Mrs. Stillwell gave me permission to talk when I wanted to talk, say nothing when I didn't want to talk, walk away, ignore people, and not worry about hurting other people's feelings. I could laugh and smile too if I felt like it. It was time to take care of myself and grieve my way for a little while.

People back at my house meant well and were trying to help, but none of them had a clue about what I was thinking and feeling. Elgin Lary and Mrs. Stillwell, on the other hand, knew what it was like to join the Grieving Parents Club and how hard it is to survive, cope, and heal after the death of a child, especially in the first couple days. They also knew me personally longer than anyone in my house, except for my parents, and they didn't waste time with pity, even in their tone of voice. They just listened, told me what to expect in the future, and told me what to do. That's what I needed to hear, and only other members of the Club could say it so empathetically and authoritatively.

Speaking with Elgin and Mrs. Stillwell gave me a little spark of life, allowed me to catch my breath, and helped me to deal with the events that followed. I didn't feel completely alone in my pain and grief anymore. It was therapeutic and allowed me to head back to the house in less of a daze. When I walked in, people were telling stories about Lexi, especially her high school friends. Girls from the cheerleading squad told silly stories about Lexi, too, and some of them actually made me laugh. It was great—it really was— but it didn't last all night.

After a while, I needed to take another break from the noise. So, I stepped out onto the front porch and just stared out into the distance again. This time, my mom, who was very teary and emotional much of the day, came out to join me. She likes to say that I was born independent, and she's right. I was extremely independent growing up, rarely needed anybody's help, and was always in control of most of what happened to me, but I needed my mom that night. I broke down and asked if she would brush and braid my hair like she did when I was a little girl, and she did. When she was done, I had two beautiful pigtails and felt like I'd been transported to a much easier time.

I know that many members of the Club turn to God for comfort and answers after the death of a child, and I grew up in a very religious and spiritual family. In fact, during the five weeks that Lexi spent battling that blood clot in the hospital, I prayed a lot. Sometimes, I'd sit alone and pray for Lexi's recovery; other times, people would come to the waiting room and invite me to pray with them. Each time Lexi came home, I was incredibly grateful and said so in prayer. But I lost interest in prayer after Lexi died.

Since Lexi died on Wednesday night, many people had approached and asked if I wanted them to pray with or for me. At first, I thought, 'Okay, sure. That's nice, but I don't know what good it's going to do. It won't bring her back." Logically, I knew and accepted that my teenaged daughter was dead, and I wasn't interested in pretending that everything was going to be okay, or that God wanted Lexi to die young for some reason. How or why could He possibly want or "will" that to happen?

I tried. I listened to the words as others prayed, but I couldn't find my own. There were no words to express how I felt, and I didn't want to put a fake smiley face on it.

After a while, I also started to get a little angry at people who said things like, "Well, God had a plan. It was her time." I didn't express it at the time, but it was building in my mind because it didn't make sense. If it was Lexi's time to die in God's plan and He had a greater purpose for her, why couldn't she have died peacefully in a hospital under heavy sedation? Why did she have to die alone in a dirt soybean field in a bloody car crash? Was I supposed to think she died in the right way because they said so? No.

One of the deputies who'd been investigating the accident came by the house on Friday night to share his findings, and they weren't comforting. He didn't get into some of the gory details at that point, and my husband Chris forbade me from reading the sheriff's report from the scene of the accident, but the basic story was pretty clear.

Lexi was driving down a country road about 7pm on June 28, 2006 when she hit a patch of recently laid loose gravel about a mile and a half from home and lost control of the car. They could tell by the skid marks that she was speeding at about 70 or 75 miles per hour when it happened. There was no posted speed limit since we lived in the country, but she was driving too fast for the conditions. They didn't know if she lost control because of the angle of the sun, a deer crossing the road, or something else, but she hit that patch of loose gravel at a high rate of speed and started to skid like she was driving on ice.

Experienced drivers know to let up on the break and turn in the direction of a skid when it happens, but Lexi had only recently become a licensed driver, and she did what most new drivers do, the opposite. She over-corrected by slamming on the brakes and steering away from skid, which sent her car careening into a utility pole on the other side of the road. The car started to flip—they could tell that it rolled two times for 85 feet into a soybean field—and Lexi wasn't wearing her seatbelt. She was thrown 80 feet out of the car through her open driver's side window and landed in the field. My baby girl was dying, bleeding to death, alone in the dirt.

Lexi's car

Accident site 1 ½ miles from home

I didn't fully emerge from a daze for a year after Lexi's death, but as time passed, I'd have lucid moments when I'd question why the accident occurred the way it did. Why was she speeding? What distracted her? Why didn't she see the gravel? Why wasn't she wearing her seatbelt when she always did it when we were together? Did she remove her seatbelt because her arm was still sore from the blood clot surgeries? I didn't ponder the cosmic question of why the accident happened at all, but I tried to piece together the sequence of events that led to it because that's how I am. Everything in my life has involved some kind of step-by-step procedure. If there's a glitch, I go back through the process, find the problem, and fix it.

I found out later from Lexi's friends that she always sped and rarely wore her seat belt. She was young and, like most teenagers, felt invincible. Maybe she didn't think she had to worry about speeding or wearing a seat belt for a short drive on an open country road. Maybe her sore arm had something to do with why she wasn't wearing a seatbelt, but I will never know for sure because there's only one person who knows, and she's not around to answer the question. She might have died anyway as the car flipped.

I wanted answers and did my research, but this was a problem that couldn't be fixed. Eventually, I realized that I was never going to find out exactly what happened and logic went out the window. Confusion and chaos hit me hard again, and now it was coupled with guilt. I was sitting on the front porch with Stasia when just over the hill on the horizon, Lexi was lying in the dirt and mud, dying. Did she wonder where her mama was? Did she cry out for me? Did she wonder why I didn't show up to help and save her? She wanted me to go with her to the church that night, but I said I was too tired. Why didn't I just go? If I had just agreed to go with her instead of working in the garden and getting some sun, she could have left earlier, wouldn't have had to drive so fast, and probably would have worn her seatbelt.

There was a lot of second guessing and associated guilt. I had nightmares about it, especially early on and even occasionally all these years later, but I've learned from other long-term, well-adjusted members of the Club that you can't live in the past, rethink every little decision, and wallow in guilt, especially when you were just doing your best under the circumstances. If you do, it will drive you insane, and that's what happens to grieving parents who don't learn to deal with guilt and live in the present.

The cruel irony that Lexi died on her way to church wasn't lost on me, either. She was so excited to see her friends in the youth group after spending most of the last five weeks in and out of the hospital. I'm not sure how religious or spiritual she really was because we never got into deep philosophical discussions about it, but she clearly loved going to church every Wednesday night to socialize, sing, pray, and learn with the people there. It was a nice, wholesome, happy group of kids who did all sorts of fun things together.

She fit in perfectly, but she didn't make it to the church that night, and she wouldn't be back.

All of this fueled my anger in the weeks and months to come, and I would need a lot more guidance and support from other members of the Club to manage it, but I wasn't there mentally or emotionally, yet.

I was still coping with the earliest stage of grief after the death of a child, and I had to focus on something else now, Lexi's funeral.

CHAPTER 5

FACING THE COLD, HARD REALITY

"Truly, it is in darkness that one finds the light, so when we are in sorrow, then this light is nearest of all to us."
— MEISTER ECKHART

This Is Not a Dream: The Visitation (July 2, 2006)

On Friday, June 30, 2006, my sisters and brothers, Holly, Cherry, Barry, Wesley, and Thomas, and some other people arrived after driving up from Texas. They found me lying in bed, still dazed and mostly staring into space. They tried to comfort and support me, but I was still trying to wrap my head around what had just happened on Wednesday night.

My family encouraged me to "get back to church" because it would be "good for me." They offered to pray with and for me and Lexi. They also wanted to talk about planning for Lexi's visitation, funeral, and burial, including the prayers, scriptures, and songs that I wanted to use during the memorial services.

I didn't stop them from praying or planning, but I didn't want to participate. I didn't want to pray anymore, and I certainly didn't want to think about planning to bury my daughter. It was the furthest thing from my mind. All I wanted to do was sit there, stare, and keep hoping and waiting to wake up from the nightmare.

Chris, my mother, and my sisters could see that I wasn't in any condition to prepare for the visitation and funeral and took care of much of it on their own. My sisters went through Lexi's closet—I hadn't gone anywhere near her room—and picked out her favorite outfit. They also found photos of Lexi, her shell necklace, earrings, makeup, and other stuff, and took it to the funeral home just in case, because Lexi's casket was going to be open at the visitation, and she had to look nice. My sister Cherry and sister-in-law Amber also took me to the mall to buy a black dress because I didn't have one.

In one of my brief lucid moments during this period, I chimed in about when we should hold the funeral. I didn't want to do it on July 2nd because that was the birthday of my nephew, London, who was just a few months younger than Stasia, and I didn't want to ruin it with sadness. I didn't want to spoil the July 4th holiday for anyone, either. So, I thought we should schedule the funeral for July 3rd, and that's what we did. It worked out perfectly.

I also insisted that someone bring Lexi's cheerleader shoes to the visitation and funeral. She had to have her shoes.

After my nephew's birthday party in the morning, Lexi's visitation took place on Sunday afternoon, July 2nd, at the funeral home in St. Joseph, IL. I arrived early with a few other family members who left me alone to grieve and pay my respects. I hadn't seen Lexi since Wednesday night, when she was lying on that stainless steel table at the hospital with only the lower half of her body visible from where I stood, but there she was, lying in a casket. I walked over to see and be with her again.

The owner of the funeral home told me to be careful about touching the left side of her face because it had been crushed and bruised in the crash, but I could hardly tell because they'd done such a good job with her reconstruction and makeup. She looked like she was sleeping peacefully, and she was so beautiful. She still looked like Lexi.

I leaned over to rest my head on her chest, but it was cold and hard. Then I touched the right side of her face, but it was even colder, and it shocked me. It literally sent a jolt of electricity through my body because I realized that *this* wasn't my Lexi. My Lexi was dead, and this wasn't a dream. The fullness of the realization didn't sink in until after her funeral, but feeling the coldness of Lexi's face and chest like that woke me up from the zombie-like trance that I'd been in for four days, and I teared up a little bit.

For the next three hours, a constant stream of people arrived at the funeral home to see Lexi for the last time. There were other family members, teenagers, and many friends from Lexi's school, church, and neighborhood, as well as friends of mine. The entire high school football team and cheerleading squad came too, and they brought Lexi's varsity letter with the cheerleading symbol on it, even though she never got to cheer.

Stasia had been playing and having a really good time at her cousin's birthday party that morning, but someone in the family brought her, too. When she came in, she went up to the casket, said "Hi, Lexi," came right back, and chastised everybody for making so much noise as they arrived and greeted each other. "Shhh. You all be quiet… My sister's sleeping." Then she went outside and played.

I was doing okay so far under the circumstances. I was tired, but I stood there as all the nice, well-meaning people came over to say how sorry they were for my loss.

The visitation had been going on for about 90 minutes when Lexi's best friend Kourtney arrived. She was trembling, having a hard time walking, and looked like she was going to faint at any moment. I walked up to her, like I'd done with Lexi's boyfriend Ryan the night of the accident, and went into nurturing mom mode. When she hesitated to approach the casket, I put my arm around her, held her arm and said, "I'll go with you." Then, she really lost it. It was heart wrenching to watch this 16-year-old girl cry so hard because she'd just lost her best friend, but I was calm.

About an hour later, there was a lull in the action because the visitation would soon be coming to an end. So, while the people who remained were conversing amongst themselves, I walked up to the casket, rested my head on Lexi's chest, felt that cold, hard shell again instead of my daughter's warm body, and for the first time since my Lexi died, sobbed uncontrollably. All of my bottled-up pain, anguish and grief erupted to the surface in a flood of tears.

It was an intense, sudden, horrific realization that I'd joined the Club. Forever.

I composed myself and went back to thanking people for showing up for the service, which continued for another half hour or so. Then I returned home to join many others who'd congregated back at the house. I went right back to my spot on the front porch and just stared out into the distance again. I was amazed at how many people loved and admired Lexi, and I was grateful to the hundreds of people who came to the visitation to pay their respects, but I was drained by three hours of sincere but somewhat robotic encounters ("thank you, thank you, thank you, thank you") and drifted back into a trance.

Cheering in Heaven: The Funeral (July 3, 2006)

We held the funeral the next morning, on the Monday before the 4th of July, at the church that Lexi was driving toward on the night that she died. Once again, my family and friends kindly coordinated with the nice people from the funeral home and took care of everything. All I had to do was show up, and I did.

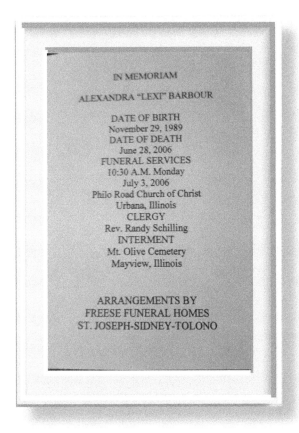

IN MEMORIAM

ALEXANDRA "LEXI" BARBOUR

DATE OF BIRTH
November 29, 1989
DATE OF DEATH
June 28, 2006
FUNERAL SERVICES
10:30 A.M. Monday
July 3, 2006
Philo Road Church of Christ
Urbana, Illinois
CLERGY
Rev. Randy Schilling
INTERMENT
Mt. Olive Cemetery
Mayview, Illinois

ARRANGEMENTS BY
FREESE FUNERAL HOMES
ST. JOSEPH-SIDNEY-TOLONO

Card from Lexi's funeral

Before the service began, I noticed that Lexi's boyfriend Ryan, who had come with his parents, was having a hard time, and I stopped thinking about me for a while. I invited him and his parents to sit right in the front with my family and me, and I kept my arm around him during the entire service that followed.

The church was full. My brothers, brothers-in-law, and many others got up to read scriptures or say a prayer. The choir sang some of Lexi's favorite gospel songs, including some that my granddaddy used to sing to her when she was child. A teddy bear that Stasia had picked out, with a ribbon that said "Sister" on it, sat near the casket. And someone had prominently displayed Lexi's cheerleading shoes on a little pedestal close to the casket. She was so proud of those shoes. They were tangible proof that she had doggedly pursued and achieved her biggest dream as a teenager.

After the church service, we all filed out into the funeral procession and drove to a cemetery about three miles from my house. Everyone stood around the casket, which was still open, as the church minister said a few words. There were flowers everywhere, and I encouraged Lexi's friends and little kids who attended to take them home.

Before they closed the casket and lowered it into the vault, I asked the funeral home people to place Lexi's cheerleading shoes in the casket, and they did. I buried those shoes with Lexi because they belonged with her for eternity, and I couldn't bear to take them away. Stasia's Teddy bear joined Lexi as well.

I come from a super-close family where everyone had died of old age in the natural course of things. When someone died, it was sad, but it was natural. Lexi's death was totally different and out of the blue. It floored me, and watching helplessly as Lexi's casket was lowered into the ground broke my heart and hurt like hell.

What Do I Do Now?

The visitation, funeral, and burial services took a toll on me, but at least I was somewhat prepared for it after my talks with Elgin and Mrs. Stillwell on Thursday. As fellow Club members, they knew what to expect, warned me that the next few days were going to test my resolve and sanity, and told me that I'd be running on pure adrenaline. They said that I should expect to crash and require plenty of rest and alone-time to recover.

As far as what to do next, my friends from the Club didn't pretend to have all of the answers and explained that there was no one-size-fits-all solution. They didn't baby me, either. They were brutally honest and basically said, "Look, here's what worked for us. You can take the advice and act on it, or you can forget it and do something else. They also reiterated that I should do whatever my mind and body were telling me to do. My grief was my own, and I shouldn't feel guilty about dealing with it in my own way.

I actually took their advice, put it into practice, and it helped a great deal.

Non-members of the Club offered all kinds of advice too, but it wasn't the same. People from the hospital and the funeral home handed out generic booklets about grief that weren't helpful. Friends from church suggested that I spend more time there, and I knew that Mrs. Stillwell had coped with her grief by immersing herself in church activities and the lives of her grandchildren, but I wasn't interested in that. Others recommended that I see a physician, therapist or professional grief counselor, read a book, take sleeping pills or anti-depressants, and well, you name it. I just listened, nodded my head, smiled (if I could), and did whatever I felt like doing or not doing.

Many people also urged me to join a secular support group of total strangers, like *Compassionate Friends*. I knew that Elgin was coping with his grief in that way and seemed to like it, but I've never liked talking with complete strangers about private affairs, mine or theirs. I'm a very outgoing person, but I compartmentalize my private and public life. I love teaching and communicating about all sorts of things, for example, but I'm very selective about whom I open up to about my feelings and private experiences, especially after Lexi's death. That makes writing this book a real departure for me.

I act differently around *real* friends, however, especially if I've known them for decades. Friends know all of your quirks, and you already know their story. And, fortunately for me, two of my old friends were members of the Club. They didn't just know Lexi and me, they knew what I was going through after Lexi's death because they'd lived through something very similar, and they knew how to talk about it with me.

Two other friends of mine who are not members of the Club, Becky Rowe and Michelle Mulcahey, also did something special for me shortly after Lexi's death that I will forever love them for.

Becky and her family rented private dorm rooms to students on the University of Illinois campus. Since it was summertime and many of the students were out of town, she called me on the Friday night after Lexi's death to do more than express her sorrow and sympathy. She said, "We have as many rooms as you need. If you have family, friends and other people coming from out of town and don't have room in your house, just tell them come here and mention your name. We will get them in. They will have a private bathroom. We'll make sure they have everything. No charge whatsoever."

It was an amazing gesture and gift. She didn't ask me how she could help or make me think. She just did it, and she explained that the rooms would be available whether I needed them or not. Well, as it turned out, some people did end up staying there.

Michelle and I had been friends for a long time too, and she knew Lexi since she was a child. We lived pretty far apart for much of our adult lives, but we stayed in touch by phone and even some old fashioned, hand-written letters. When she called after Lexi's death, we hadn't seen each other in person in a few years, but it didn't matter. She said, "I'm going to be there," and she was. She left her two young children with her husband, flew all the way from Atlanta, Georgia, attended the visitation and funeral, and returned home. I couldn't believe that she came on such short notice and told her so. She just said, "I needed to be there for you."

Michelle didn't ask me if I wanted her to come or even make me think about it. She just did it. She showed up. Like Becky, she made an executive decision to help in a specific way and took the pressure off of me when I couldn't handle any more. I didn't need to have a plan for Michelle and Becky, and I will always love and appreciate them for it.

Over the ten years since Lexi's death, I've reached out to other grieving parents in my area and in my own way, much as Elgin and Mrs. Stillwell helped me in the beginning. I did because I want them to have at least one person who isn't walking on eggshells, treating them with kid gloves, and looking at them with those pitiful eyes after the death of their child. Only members of the Club, especially old-timers like me, understand how to properly welcome newcomers, as awful as it is.

Sometimes, it works the other way around, and grieving parents reach out to me. Recently, another mother of a teenaged girl who was killed in an auto accident contacted me. She had read a newspaper article about one of my speeches to high school students about safe driving and Lexi's death. She told me this very touching story.

Her husband was a police officer who had signed up for an overtime detail to make some extra money before the fatal accident occurred, but he couldn't do it after his daughter died because there was suddenly a flurry of higher priority things to take care of. Well, without asking how he could help, one of her husband's colleagues on the squad took his overtime shift and then, a couple days later, send a card to them with the overtime money. It wasn't a ton of money, but it didn't matter. It was such a kind, thoughtful gesture by somebody who just helped out by trying to make their life a tiny bit easier without expecting anything in return.

Like Becky and Michelle, he took the initiative. He just did it.

That kind of empathic response means a great deal to a grieving parent, especially during the first week, and you don't have to be a member of the Club to understand why.

CHAPTER 6

ALONE AGAIN, NATURALLY
(SURVIVING THE MILESTONES)

"Surround yourself with the people who love you,
and know that you are not alone."

– Molly Tarlov

The Sound of Silence

The number of visitors slowly started decreasing for a couple days after Lexi's funeral. Then there was a mass exodus. By the time a week had passed, only my mom and dad were still around. That was pretty much it. Everybody else went back to work, school, vacations, and their regular lives, and that's the way it is.

The constant white noise of conversation and moving parts that sometimes irritated me over the past week was replaced with the sound of silence. I could literally hear the crickets chirping. If we had tumble weeds in eastern Illinois, I'm sure I would have heard them, too, because the sudden contrast was so striking. The food disappeared, the flowers faded and died, and almost everyone left.

Even when I had to get away from the house and the noise in the past, it comforted me to know that there would be lots of people around when I returned. Human beings are social creatures who normally like to be around other people. We like our solitude at times, but not for too long. Now I had to adapt to a sudden change in my surroundings. I was still trying to handle not having Lexi around every day, and now—boom—everyone else was gone. The silence shocked my system. I didn't even hear the sounds of cars driving down the road anymore.

The quiet of the night, when the birds weren't singing joyfully and everyone else was asleep, bothered me the most. When I had people around to keep me from thinking too hard about Lexi's death, my nights were hard but tolerable. Now, the people were gone, and the quiet of the night scared me to death.

I should have called my friends in the Club again right away, but I didn't, and I paid a heavy price for it. I wasn't used to this brand-new life as a member of the Club and mistakenly decided that I could deal with this new quiet phase (and the anger that came with it) on my own. It may have been quiet around me, but it was not that way in my head. I became increasingly angry at other human beings, especially other parents who didn't have to grieve like this, friends and family who weren't in the Club but kept giving me advice, and most of all, at God for allowing this to happen at all.

I had been able to deal with and control my emotions my entire life, but not anymore. Not in this phase. I couldn't do it, but I was too proud and stubborn to contact anyone from the Club who had gone through the same things in the past. I thought I could handle it on my own, and I didn't want to talk with anyone while I was so angry, bitter, and hateful. I didn't want to bring any of my friends or family down with me, and I didn't want to be known as a person who's always complaining and never calls just to say "Hi" and have a few laughs.

I told myself that all it took was willpower, but I was wrong. It's hard for me to admit that I was wrong about something like this in those early days, but I was. And, without guidance from other Club members during this phase, the smallest things set me off like they never had before. The "why" questions ("Why Lexi?" "Why me?"

"Why now?") set me into a rage. If anger, fear, jealousy, and hatred are the path to the dark side, and as a Star Wars geek, I think they are… I was quickly walking down that path.

Just Give Me the Drugs

Lexi, like many other teenaged girls, used to change her clothes twenty times before finding the right outfit, and she probably did it again before she left to meet her friends at the church youth group on the night she died. There were clothes here, there, and everywhere, all over her bedroom. She hadn't made her bed, and the whole room was a pig sty.

It took me three or four weeks to even bring myself to open the door. I just stood there, peeked in, and cried. Everything was just as she left it because I'd instructed everyone not to touch her stuff, clean up, or mess with anything. I finally let my mom clean up in there a bit. I said she could make the bed, pack things up, and put things back in closets and drawers, as long as she didn't throw anything away. I wouldn't let her wash anything, though; so many things still had the scent of Lexi's favorite perfume.

Family and friends who encountered me during this period could tell that I wasn't my normal silly, easygoing self and advised me to get some counseling or therapy. My mood and demeanor had changed dramatically, and I couldn't sleep. This went on for weeks, and it started to take its toll on me physically. I was falling apart. Eventually, I became so exhausted from lack of sleep and mental anguish that I agreed to try different anti-anxiety drugs, antidepressants, and sleeping aids.

I made an appointment with my primary care physician, Dr. Lee, who had also been Lexi's doctor. After prescribing something to help me sleep, she told me that I really needed to see a trained therapist who knew more about pharmacological fixes for grief, depression, anxiety, insomnia, and the like, and she offered to help me find one. Then, about a month after Lexi's funeral, I finally did it. I went to see a psychiatrist for the first time, mainly because I wanted stronger drugs.

On my first visit to her office, the psychiatrist listened to me and said, "Well, I think we need to get you a few sessions. We really need to figure out why you're so sad and angry." That was it. I lost it. I yelled at her, "Are you effing kidding me? I see all of those diplomas, but are you some kind of idiot? I know exactly why I'm angry and sad. My daughter was killed, okay? Just give me drugs. I don't need to spend hours and money trying to figure out why I'm so sad and angry." I got the prescription and walked out.

I took the drugs, didn't feel any better, and went back to my primary care physician to find out why. She recommended that I go back to a specialist for another prescription because the drugs I was taking clearly weren't working. They were meant to calm me down, but I was bouncing off the walls at 3 o'clock in the morning, as if my body was rejecting them and rebelling in overdrive. Instead of relaxing and putting me to sleep, the drugs were making me feel like I'd just drunk five cups of espresso. Trying not to wake anyone, I would be on my hands and knees in the wee hours of the morning scrubbing the concrete floors in my basement utility room because I could take out my frustrations there without waking anyone upstairs.

Since I'd insulted the intelligence of my first psychiatrist and all of her ancestors, I couldn't go back there, and honestly, I didn't want to. I felt like she wanted to psychoanalyze everything about me. Perhaps that helps people who have deep-seated issues or repressed memories and such, but I felt that anybody with a lick of common sense would be able to see what was going on. It was like she was reading from a script, like some telemarketer, and she wasn't going to deviate from it. My child was dead! That was it. If she couldn't see that, I was never again going to waste my time and money with her. So I went to a psychologist the next time, but the result was the same. He opened with, "Let's see if we can figure out why you're so angry," after which

I cussed him out, questioned whether or not he had any brain cells, grabbed my prescription, and walked out in a huff.

Therapists may help some people, but I thought they were stupid. I knew exactly why I was angry and sad. It wasn't my mother, my father, or some repressed memory. My teenage daughter had died, and it happened suddenly. There was no need to delve into my psyche and "id." The cause of my grief was obvious. The whole thing was moronic to me.

My primary care physician was amazed that I continued to function day-to-day under the circumstances. I shouldn't have even been driving, but I was. I got up each day, took Stasia to preschool, ran errands, visited the cemetery, went to work (driving miles out of my way to avoid seeing the flowers left by friends as a memorial by the utility pole that Lexi hit), and taught 4 or 5 classes. I did it all, but I was miserable and tired all the time. Before walking into my classroom to teach once again, I stopped in front of the door, took a deep breath and did my best to prevent my students from knowing what I was going through. I quickly learned how to fake a smile and act like everything was okay when it wasn't.

Approximately eight weeks passed between my first two visits with a therapist and my next one. I went back for different drugs, and that's all, but whatever I took either didn't work at all, or it had the opposite effect on me. Some even made me delusional or paranoid. Others brought on hallucinations. We must have tried about fifteen different kinds of drugs over an 8-week period. We didn't talk about anything else because I thought he was an idiot. I'd go in, say hello, and stay long enough for him to write out a new prescription. The whole thing normally took no longer than 15 minutes.

I was emotional, and yes, their comments about figuring out the source of my "anger" hit a nerve. They knew that my daughter had died. I had told them time and time again. It was in their notes, but they didn't seem to want to address it directly, which only made me angrier. I know I needed help. I wasn't sleeping or eating. I wasn't focused. The "professionals" were not helping me, though. After a while, I would sit with a counselor almost as a matter of principle, and really only to get a prescription for something (anything) that would make my world normal again.

I probably saw twelve different counselors, therapists, social workers, psychologists, and psychiatrists in the first year and a half after Lexi died. I tried every kind of drug to alleviate or mitigate my anxiety, depression, and anger, but nothing worked. I finally reached the point where I was sleeping only about two hours a day. My body became accustomed to it, but I knew it wasn't healthy, and my weight went from around 140 pounds to about 120 pounds.

Now, ten years later, I still have absolutely no desire to go to "professional" counseling. Could it help? It's possible, but at this point, I still feel like they all read from the same script. Just because it doesn't work for me, though, doesn't mean counseling couldn't work for others. There really is no one-size-fits-all!

Fortunately, I didn't wait a year and a half to reach out to other Club members for more guidance because, as usual, it prepared me to cope with the grief to come in the months and the holiday season to come.

The Waves of Grief

I waited too long to reach out to friends in the Club, but I finally called Elgin and Mrs. Stillwell again in the fall, a few months after the funeral. Once again, they offered advice that no one else was willing or able to offer.

First, they assured me that my anger and strong negative emotions were perfectly normal during this early stage of the grieving process. Even the nicest, sweetest people who suffer the death of a child can go to the dark side from time to time. New members start having time alone with their thoughts, and they begin to more fully realize what just happened. It's like having a bloody scrape on your arm or your knees after you fall down. Even after it starts to heal, it's still ready to bleed again at even the slightest touch. Early stage grief after the death of a child is equally raw. New members of the Club are still in a daze, but the slightest thing can set off the synapses and nerve endings of their grief.

Second, they told me to get used to feeling an intense sense of loneliness when everyone goes home after an event because you'll wonder if you're the only person who's ever felt like this when you're alone with your thoughts again. You are not alone—there are so many other Club members who will empathize with, guide, and help you. They have felt the same way. New members of the Club just don't realize it yet, which is why it's so important to continue reaching out to other grieving parents in the months and years to come.

Third, they said that I should expect to feel numb most of the time during the first year, as if I was walking in slow motion. Since then, I've heard people describe it as our mind's way of giving grieving parents a bit of a break to heal and recover during this stage, and it certainly turned out to be true in my case. There was numbness combined with rawness; I started putting one foot in front of the other, but the grief always returned in waves, as if I was standing with my back to the ocean and my eyes closed. Some of the waves would lap at my heels and barely register; others would hit like a tsunami, pull me out to sea, and would have sucked the life out of me if I wasn't ready for them.

Fourth, they warned me that the holidays, Lexi's birthday (November 29), and other milestones were coming up fast and going to be particularly hard to handle, especially in the first year when she would be conspicuously missing from the festivities. Other things —a song, a sound, a sign, a person, you name it—would trigger unexpected waves of grief, too. How I chose to remember my child and recognize the holidays and milestones was totally up to me because there was no right or wrong way.

Thanks to help and guidance from these Club members, I was more or less prepared for the major milestones to come around the holidays and beyond. It was hard, of course, but I didn't fall apart. I kept myself really busy with work, projects, and errands because I knew that just around the corner, thinking about Lexi was going to be painful.

I bought balloons, flowers, a birthday card, and a little present for Lexi on her birthday, which we celebrated on Thanksgiving like we did every year. Since she preferred pumpkin pie to cake, I baked a pumpkin pie and put her name on a slice of it in icing. Then we took it down to the cemetery, dug a hole near the grave, and put the pie in there along with her birthday card, and talked with her. It was heartbreaking, and I cried a lot when Stasia couldn't see me, but it built up my immune system, much like you take more vitamin C than usual before cold and flu season. I steeled myself for the worst.

At Christmas, my parents did something special that really made a difference for me. We usually spent Christmas together as a family at my parent's home in Ft. Worth, Texas. This year, my mom and dad wisely rented a house in Austin, Texas, about 4 hours away from their house. If we had congregated at my parent's place as usual, I wouldn't have been able to look at anything without being reminded of Lexi and my grandfather, Harlan, who had passed away in October. Nothing in that vacation house was familiar; it was very helpful.

Even though I was sort of prepared for the major milestones, little ones really snuck up on me. For example, while I was standing in the middle of a Walmart that fall looking at books and other back-to-school supplies, my eyes fixated on a bottle of Elmer's school glue, and I totally lost it. I burst into tears, with my shoulders heaving and all that, because Lexi and I always hit the back-to-school sales together. Even when she was a teenager, we'd go out every year to get some new, cool outfits, a backpack, a trapper keeper, and all the school supplies. Now, since Stasia wasn't in school yet, I had nobody to join me for some back-to-school shopping. Something I had done for years and years and years was over, and a wave of loss hit me like a brick out of the blue.

The following year, I knew that back-to-school shopping bothered me and prepared myself to deal with it differently. I didn't pretend it wasn't happening. I went back to the store, bought every product that I'd normally buy and more—I must have purchased 20 bottles of glue and 500 pencils—and donated all of it to charity. I knew that one way to deal with it was to trick my brain into thinking back-to-school shopping was happening like it normally does, and it worked. I filled up a whole bunch of those fill-the-bag, pack-in items they have for lower-income students in the area, and it felt good.

I give my students test-taking tips. A lot of people get test "quake" when they stare at the first question of a test. Their mind goes blank, and they freak out. They can avoid this, however, by playing a trick on their brain at the outset. All they have to do is flip a few pages and start on question number 20 rather than question number one. The brain will act as if they've already successfully answered 19 questions and kick right into gear. That's what I do in other situations, like those back-to-school shopping trips by myself: I trick my brain into thinking all is well, and I do it every year now.

I've also learned that doing things for others helps Club members to cope, especially when we help others in honor and memory of our departed children. Not only does it make us feel good; it keeps us busy, and that's important, especially in the first year or so. We need someone else to think about.

Whatever a new member of the Club decides is most helpful in coping with grief, aside from obviously self-destructive coping mechanisms like suicide or addiction, is perfectly fine. I chose to bury a slice of pumpkin pie on the first birthday after Lexi died, and it's become a yearly tradition. I make pumpkin pie; I write a birthday card; I buy flowers; we sing happy birthday to Lexi; and I take everything to the cemetery and put it near her grave. We hang a Christmas stocking up for Lexi every year, and I always buy her a special ornament. Some Club members don't do these things, and that's fine. How a member chooses to remember their deceased children is a purely private matter.

Stasia to the Rescue

Six or seven months after Lexi's funeral, I went to see my primary care physician again for more antidepressants, and she gave me some useful advice under the circumstances, especially for someone who isn't a member of the Club. She said, "Okay Kelly. Talking to people just doesn't work for you, but you need to get your feelings out somehow. So write a letter to everybody who said something hurtful to you. Write a letter to God and tell him how pissed off you are. Then burn them."

I liked that idea and did it for a while. It felt great getting it off my chest and on paper, but I didn't stop there. I started banging out angry songs on my piano. I even went out and yelled at trees once in a while. It made me feel at little better and became my way of getting these dark feelings out in the open since I wasn't comfortable with talking to people about my problems and didn't want to burden anyone else with them.

I almost completely stopped talking to my husband Chris, who just went to work each day and tried to keep busy and avoid a confrontation with me. We both wanted to protect Stasia from what was going on. So, we didn't go around the house crying, sobbing, or arguing, and we didn't build a shrine to Lexi the house. In fact, we didn't change anything in Lexi's bedroom. We kept Stasia on schedule, with pre-school and her friends coming and going as usual, and it worked. As far as she was concerned, everything was fine.

I felt so much guilt about failing Lexi as a mother, and I was determined not to screw up Stasia's life too. I thought about it every time I looked at her, and it gave my life purpose.

Even when I took Stasia to visit Lexi's grave, I kept smiling and tried not to cry. As a result, Stasia thought the cemetery was the most beautiful place in the world, with pretty rocks and flowers everywhere. It was always a happy place for her. She used to sit with me on a little bench in front of another teenage girl's grave. The girl's grandparents had built it, and they graciously allowed us to use it. Stasia would sit there and pretend she was watching TV and movies and just let her imagination run wild.

Stasia is almost thirteen years old now, and she knows how much I love her, but she doesn't know that she saved my life after Lexi died just by being my cute, lovable three-year old girl. If I didn't have Stasia, I most likely wouldn't have made it through the first few weeks. She helped Chris and me cope during this difficult, lonely, and dark phase of the grieving process when I foolishly didn't reach out to other members of the Club for guidance and wasn't interested in talking to or hearing from anyone else.

Stasia at 3 years-old;

Stasia, kindergarten picture day with photo of her big sister;

Stasia, 7th grade, 2016

Not Going Back in Black

When the first year anniversary of Lexi's death arrived on June 28, 2007, I decided to celebrate it in my own way. As I mentioned earlier, I bought a black dress shortly before Lexi's visitation because I didn't own one. I wore that polyester dress to Lexi's visitation and funeral. I wore it again to my maternal grandfather's funeral in October and to my paternal grandfather's memorial service in early June. They both basically died of a broken heart because they couldn't imagine a world where you outlive your great-grandchild. Well, I went out to the backyard, dipped it in kerosene, lit a match, and watched it burn, throwing in some dried sage in an effort to "purify" my surroundings. I watched the flames grow and consume that sadness-filled dress, inhaled the earthy scent of the sage, and I actually felt moments of peace. In a way, during those brief moments, I was saying goodbye to the "old" me and accepting the "new" me. People have always had rituals to mark beginnings and endings. These rites help us cope and make sense of change, and allow us to feel like we have some sense of control over the uncontrollable. This was my personal ritual, and it did make me feel like I was in control —even though it was just for a few moments.

I've been in the Club for ten years now, and as I look back on my first year after Lexi died, I can assure new members who feel the same type of strong negative emotions, rawness, numbness, loneliness, and unexpected waves of grief that they're not crazy. It's normal to experience these things, as painful, uncomfortable, and disturbing as they are. You'll know that's true if you talk to another member of the Grieving Parents Club when the funeral for your loved one is over and everyone goes home. Members are the most generous, kind-hearted, understanding people in the world. They don't care if everyone else is tired of your complaining and whining and crying because they're not. So, don't make my mistake of waiting months after my daughter's funeral to reach out to other members and ask for help and guidance. When I finally did it, they were there for me, as always.

If you can't find another member of the Club to talk to and express your feelings, write them down; yell at a rock, a tree, or a squirrel (rather than a family member or friends). Find other ways to voice your feelings that work for you. You don't have to share your feelings with another person if you don't want to, but you've got to get them out before they fester too long inside of you.

Speaking the Unspeakable

Too many friends and family members disappear after a child's funeral and avoid new members of the Club, as if our grief is contagious or speaking with us is always going to be uncomfortable because you don't want to talk or think about death. Well, if you know and love that person, don't disappear after their child is buried. You can make a difference for a grieving parent with a friendly email, letter, or note. Better yet, stop by or meet us for some coffee. Invite us to join you for a walk or an event. We need to keep busy during that first year, especially in the first few months.

When the numbness subsides, we want to talk about our child again and appreciate the opportunity to do so. If you're avoiding us because you don't want to make us sad by bringing up our child's name, there's no need for that. You're not going to make us sad because we never forget that our child has passed away. We're aware of it in every waking moment, even when we're laughing and smiling. We know that you're busy, but we want to know that we still matter to the people in our lives, and we can't help but notice when others distance themselves from us emotionally and physically.

Other grieving parents talking about our children don't make us uncomfortable, but non-members often don't handle it well. We're sorry about that, but if you want to help, show up during those quiet times. Text us, email us, send us a card, stop by, and if it still makes you uncomfortable, simply say, "I was just thinking about you." That's all you have to say so that we know that we're not alone.

Most non-members are kindhearted and well-meaning but fall back on clichés when they don't know what to say, and I get tired of those. They try to use these well-worn clichés and sayings, things that they've heard before. They are trying to fix us. We can't be fixed. These sayings don't help us; they actually hurt us. We may smile, but only because we don't want to cause a scene by getting angry, yelling, or crying.

So, don't say things like, "Time heals all wounds." I still hear this. This is a wound that doesn't heal. Time may stem some of the bleeding, but it is a very open wound. We can do things; we can put a bandage on it, but the wound is always there. The wound is never going to completely heal over. The wound was created by a combination of love and loss. If it ever completely healed over, that would mean that we didn't remember. Instead of saying a cliché, just let us know you're thinking about us: you wanted to say hi, ask if we need anything.

Please don't say, "Let go; move on." Somebody actually said that to me. They said, "We're really sorry that you're having such a hard time getting over the death of Lexi. You need to move on, get back to church and things like ...." Everybody grieves; when you lose a beloved pet, when you lose a spouse, a parent, yes it's grief, but a child to a parent is the most precious asset.

It's the most precious thing in the world, and then they're gone. As long as we remember our children (and that's really all we want to do), we can't let go and move on. To move on means to put everything in the past, to put it in storage. You want to help us when we struggle? Ask about our child; ask for stories. Let us know; don't tell us to move on. After a while, you get tired of being nice and putting a polite smile on your face, and you just want to say, "Okay, so after one of your children dies, what's the good time limit? How would you feel?"

There's No Need to Speculate about *Why*

Unless you can tell me exactly why Lexi was killed in a horrible car wreck after having spent all those weeks in a hospital, do not say, "It happened for a reason." Don't even try, because I'm going to ask you, "What's the good reason for one of your children to die?" Children should never, ever die before their parents and grandparents and great-grandparents. There may be a cause, but there is not a reason. You cannot give us one. The same goes for, "God had a plan." Unless you can tell me the exact plans, step by step, don't say, "God needed her (or him)." I'm pretty sure if there is an omnipotent deity, they didn't need my child at that time. Just try saying, "I'm sorry, I'm here if you need me."

I don't care how religious and spiritual someone was before joining the Club; there is still a part of them that is asking why. Intelligent human beings with free will ask, "Why?" Unless you have the answer to that, don't go there. Just don't. Don't say, "At least you had her for 16 years," or "At least you have other children." I've heard this said so many times. After you hear that about three dozen times, you want to lash out and shout back, "Okay, how many years are good for you? You have other children; great. Which other children are you willing to bury? You have others."

Again, I understand because I used to be this way; I used to say the same things, but you don't realize. Actually don't ever say anything to a grieving parent that starts with, "At least da, da, da," Just don't.

It's the Thought that Counts

Just ask us about our children. Ask us about a funny story; what they were like and things like that. We cherish opportunities to talk about them, especially if you can refrain from offering unsolicited advice about coping with the death of a child. In fact, when people say or suggest that we should stop talking about our child, forget about our child, or just put it in the past and move on, we get a little sad. At least, I do. Here's the thing: We may smile, we may laugh, and we may joke, but inside we're sad, and we're going to stay that way until the day we die.

We are painfully aware of the fact that they're gone. Every single moment talking, sharing memories, tears, and laughter, doesn't make us any more or less sad. We don't want to act like our child never existed. My Lexi existed, and I want people to know she was awesome.

I recently had a very interesting visit from a former student. She is a very special lady to me, an older woman. She had come here years and years ago from Honduras, legally, the right way, with her family, and she had been my student in several classes. Her English is not so good. My Spanish is not as good as it should be. Yet, we still were able to bond and become close. She had gone through the naturalization process, and she had specifically asked if I would be her guest when she became an American citizen. Of course, I was thrilled to do that.

We had a teacher/student relationship, but we also had a respect and a great fondness for each other, and I know what a hard worker she is. One day, she knocked on my office door and just wanted to let me know that she was in the neighborhood and that she had been praying for me. She just hugged me, tears in her eyes, and said, "You're such a special lady, and I want you to know God had a plan for taking Lexi. I brought you a couple of books." I have them here in my office still. She's very religious and very active in her local Catholic parish. I really appreciated it.

The religious stuff bothered me at first, but the fact that she drove out of her way, that she came up here and took time off from work just to see me and let me know that she was thinking about me kind of superseded everything else.

I just gave her a big hug. I thanked her. I told her how much I appreciated her telling me that she was thinking about me. The whole "God has a plan" thing didn't really help me, and it really wasn't what I needed to hear, but it wasn't a cliché to her. It wasn't something to say because you don't know what else to say. She really believed this, and she wanted to let me know as a way to comfort. So, that's different from other people who just use the same clichés.

It didn't set me off. It was special. It's the thought that counts, and hers definitely did.

CHAPTER 7

THE LAST DAMN BRIDGE

"Don't give up. Don't ever give up."

— JIM VALVANO

After the "Firsts": Year Two and Beyond

After a while, when your friends and family have gone back to their regular lives, you're going to face a lot of firsts. There's the first birthday without your child, the first Christmas or Hanukkah, the first Easter, 4th of July, and the first anniversary of their death. It's going to be hard, but you'll survive with a little help from other Club members. You'll also begin to figure out the little things that set you off and anticipate how you're going to feel. Slowly but surely, you'll start to become more comfortable with the milestones and adjust to your new normal, which will include some behaviors and activities from your old life.

Some of the waves that hit you after the first year will be humongous and knock the living daylights out of you, but the big waves start coming in less frequently as the years pass. When they do come in, they hit you HARD, but they do start coming in less frequently. You still have the constant smaller waves of grief, but you can stand your ground with them. You can survive them. Some of the waves are going to bring a tear to your eye, but some are also going to bring laughter.

"The Last Damn Bridge" to me is a metaphor for life. It doesn't necessarily get any easier, but you are better able to steel yourself and prepare. Last fall, more than nine years after Lexi died, I ran the New

York City Marathon, my very first full marathon. It was hard. It was long. I totally did not prepare for it as I should have. There were five bridges. In fact, the first bridge is the starting line, called Verrazano-Narrows Bridge. Running coaches and training programs will tell you that you've got to train for those first two miles because the bridge has got this high incline and is very long. That bridge wasn't the problem, though. It was the other four bridges.

You get going. You get into a rhythm. You have the long first two miles of the Verrazano-Narrows Bridge out of Staten Island, then twelve miles in Brooklyn. It's nice and flat and everybody's cheering. You get your pace, and you kind of get your groove… And then you hit a bridge. The pavement's different. The elevation is awful. I was just getting into a routine, and then I'd hit a bridge. You get into the routine again, and after sixteen miles, you hit the Queensboro Bridge. That one was probably the toughest for me, and for many others.

Then at mile twenty, you hit the last of the five bridges, the Willis Avenue Bridge. When I arrived, I noticed a lady standing there near the Bronx with the most honest and awesome sign I had ever seen in a race. None of this, "Oh, you're almost there. You're doing great!" It simply said, "The Last Damn Bridge."

Last Damn Bridge

Hundreds of runners were so happy at that point to have reached the last of these horrible bridges. It was the last one to cross. We were chanting, "The last damn bridge!" I mean, we all cheered. We got our second wind. We were skipping and singing, and the runners were all dancing and chanting, "Last damn bridge." We knew exactly what "last damn bridge" meant. I don't think the lady holding the sign had run before. If not, she couldn't know exactly how much we appreciated that sign and what a lift it gave us.

The problem was, it was still 6.2 miles uphill to the finish line in Central Park. During those last miles, I hit "The Wall." Everything is hurting. Your body does not want to go on anymore. I still had 6.2 miles to go, uphill, but even so, I was motivated because I didn't have any more of those horrible high elevation bridges.

As I was thinking about it, it really did become a metaphor for life. My journey was not over by any stretch of the imagination. I still had 6.2 miles to go, uphill. My legs hurt. My feet hurt. My mind was saying that I was crazy, but I couldn't give up. I had survived those five bridges. 6.2 miles was nothing compared to hitting those bridges, and I thought that's kind of how life is. The early milestones, the "firsts," those are like your bridges. When you cross them and you survive, it's a big relief. You get a little breathing room there. Then all of a sudden, another milestone hits, and that's another bridge.

At some point, you've gone through all the firsts. Or you've gone through major milestones in life, and you will forever be grieving. Not crying, but you'll always be grieving for your child. Life is going to still be tough. You've still got the 6.2 miles uphill, but you made it over some things that life just threw at you. New York marathon runners have those five bridges, and just as they can survive, you can survive.

If you can make it over those five bridges, if you can make it past the last damn bridge, you're going to have good times, you're going to have bad times, but you can do it. That's what it meant to me. It really is a good metaphor. You could quit right then, but why would you quit when you've survived super hard stuff? The tsunami, the tidal waves of emotions—they are your bridges and your hills.

There is happy stuff on the way. There are so many people cheering you on those last 6.2 miles. There's a great medal and poncho and food. There is such a feeling of strength. So, you can do it. You don't have to give up.

I did it!! I survived my first marathon.

There's an important distinction between a "Last Damn Bridge" sign and another sign saying, "You're Almost There." The people holding signs and cheering about how it's almost over and trying to distract you from reality and your pain are kind of like non-members of the Club. They want to help and cheer you on, but they don't know exactly what to say. Someone holding a "Last Damn Bridge" sign shows the honesty, empathy, and humor that Club members love and appreciate. The person holding that sign wasn't making any false promises or sugar-coating anything. This is the last damn bridge.

I actually remember seeing one of those "You're Almost There" signs at mile 3 in Brooklyn, and I knew I still had more than 23 miles, many of them uphill, in front of me. I wasn't almost there. I was a lot closer to the starting line than the finish line. And when a runner like me sees a sign like that so early in the race, we tend to think, "Yeah, whatever."

In my personal experience, in some ways, I don't know if I'm there or maybe I missed the sign for my last damn bridge. Maybe psychologically I'm still waiting for another one. But in other ways, I think I have crossed it.

I think my very last bridge will be making it through the 10-year anniversary of Lexi's death this summer, June 28, 2016, because "10" years is a psychological milestone. Everything expected and unexpected, with her friends getting married, having babies, having careers, families; everything that generally can happen that might set me off has happened. And so I think, if I can just make it through this 10 year mark, it might be my last damn bridge.

I'm not saying it's going to get a lot easier, but I will know that I can survive and I can handle pretty much anything.

I think it's the number 10. Even in birthdays, the major birthdays end in 5s or 0s. A 9-year anniversary, an 11-year anniversary is not as common to hear about, but 10, it's that round number that has stuck in my head. It was the 5th anniversary when I started running as kind of "me time."

I had a hard time doing things. It was after the 5th anniversary, I started my doctoral program. That I started running. These were things that became very positive in my life.

As I got closer to this 10, it was tough, and so I'm doing other things to help me help others, so I think this is the perfect time.

How to Cope and Heal after Your Last Damn Bridge

How do you continue running those last 6.2 miles after you've hit and crossed your personal Last Damn Bridge? As always, you should go with whatever works best for you, as long as it's not self-destructive, and you should turn to other members of the Club whenever you need them along the way. But that doesn't mean there aren't certain ways of coping and healing after the Last Damn Bridge that tend to commonly work for Club members. So, let's talk about them.

- ## Accept and Acknowledge Your Grief, Guilt, Doubt, and Demons

Once you cross your Last Damn Bridge, it really comes down to accepting and acknowledging your grief, guilt, doubt, and demons. Of course, that is often a lot easier said than done. It happened to me when I crossed mine. Psychologically, I thought, "Yes!" I hate bridges. I live in East Central Illinois. We don't even have hills, let alone bridges. It's flat.

I was never athletic. I was never into sports. That was always my siblings. I always thought it was this made-up, coach, pep-talk thing. "Play with your heart. Play with your mind." That was a lot of motivational mumbo-jumbo to me. But these fellow runners said, "No, you will actually feel it when you've hit the wall. About mile 20 to 22, you will meet your demon." They described it as demon instead of wall because what it does to you is ugly.

And I hit it. I made it past the last damn bridge. I was doing well for another mile, but at mile 21, I hit my wall, and I saw the scariest demon. My thought was, I could quit right now. I had nothing more to give. But I summoned up everything I had, and I said to my demon, "Screw you! I'm going to crawl the last five miles if I have to, but you're not stopping me." It was like the demon was going to stop me from crossing the bridge, and I simply said, "Not happening."

I acknowledged it was tough. I acknowledged there was pain. I could have quit and taken it easy, but I didn't. Acknowledge that your grief is real, and it's okay. It's okay to have good days and bad days. You're going to have guilt. You're going to have dark times. You're going to have whatever you want to refer to it as: demons, a wall, darkness, or even loss of faith. It's going to try and keep you from taking another step forward and living your life.

If you listen to other grieving parents that have fought off their Wall and their Demon, you can see that there is hope. You're going to have dark times, but they don't last forever. I admit that I don't have all the answers. I acknowledge that without reaching out to other people and without getting some help, I wouldn't be where I am. Sometimes, you need a shoulder, whether it's a literal or figurative shoulder, to lean on, to get you through the demons and the dark times.

"Why" questions are particularly tough, and often they are the first questions that are ever asked. It happens a lot. I still ask it. I still ask it because I haven't gotten an answer. Why my child? Why any child? Why do good people die? Why do bad things happen to good people? Sometimes the "why" relates to a specific child. But sometimes it evolves into a question larger than just the child. "Why do bad things happen to good people?" In most cases, there's just not an answer. But human beings are a curious species. We ask why.

I remember when Lexi was little, just starting to talk at 1 and a half or 2 years old, everything was why. "Why? Why? Why? Why? Why?" We don't lose that when we become adults. Sometimes, we just accept the fact that we don't have an answer. But little children are always asking why. It's natural to wonder why. It's natural to seek out an answer. It's not as ever-present as time goes on. Even for people that are deeply spiritual and religious, it's natural. All the people in the Bible questioned God, right? It is perfectly natural.

It's okay to ask why. It's okay to question God. At Lexi's visitation, there was a Catholic priest who was coming through the line, and I didn't know him, but he was just paying his respects. He went over to my mother. My mother asked him why. He said, "Well, God has a plan." She told him that wasn't good enough. I watched, and my sisters were eavesdropping and told me later that my mother was having a really hard time. Lexi was the oldest, the first grandchild. I'm the oldest child. The priest had started off with the cliché answer but then sat down and he said, "You know what, let's take this a different way.

"A lot of people will say, 'Jesus died too.' And Mary was asking why. People will always say God had a plan, God had a plan. He said, at the time, Mary didn't know why. She didn't know what was going to happen. All she knew was that her son was dead." Something in that sparked a change in my mom. She got some kind of answer that made sense to her. You know, this was from a Catholic priest, and I didn't grow up Catholic, but it's okay to ask why. It is perfectly okay. The mother of Jesus asked why.

But after the accident, people told me I needed to pray. "You need to pray for strength." "You need to pray for peace in your heart." I was angry. I thought the car wreck was the answer to my prayers. And I asked why a lot. People said, "It's a mystery of life." "There's a plan." I started having doubts. I've had people tell me, "Kelly, you really need to try." And honestly, I have. However, I've come to the conclusion that I'm not going to rely on some mythical entity to fix things. If anybody is going to fix me, it's going to be me. And that's just my stubbornness and independence. But I've tried.

I'm still really angry because of the chain of events. If there was this great cosmic plan, that it was her time, why couldn't she have gone peacefully under heavy medication at the hospital? Why did it have to be so… so vicious? That chain of events still makes me angry.

It's whatever you need at a given point in time.

If you have a personality like mine, you really do have to realize that you're not weak just because you need help. It is not negative. It's not a forever thing. I saw a picture of the Boston Marathon, and in it, someone's body was giving out, and two of the other runners came up and put themselves under the first's arms and helped them finish it. Sometimes, even the strongest people trip, and you just need a little help until you can get back on your feet, and then you can go on.

I don't ever want to come across as insulting people who are very religious or who are very spiritual. I know lots of grieving parents, and it works for them. At this point in my life, it doesn't work for me, but I find other ways to be strong.

• Let Others Help You

Like a lot of people, I'm a very stubborn, independent, and private person. I don't like asking others for help for anything. My parents said that even as a small child, I wanted to do everything myself. I always thought that asking other people for help was a sign of weakness. I have learned it's not. It's actually courageous to ask other people to help you. It takes strength.

Here are some people that helped me throughout this process.

o Members of the Grieving Parents Club

One goal of this book is to let grieving parents know that you don't have to do this alone. We all need a little help sometimes; other parents are there to help you. We can't do your journey for you, and you may get battered and bruised in your new journey, but you don't have to face your battles alone. You do not have to fight alone.

Other members of the Grieving Parents Club are there for you. I'm here for you. Lots of people are willing to pick you up when you trip to help you fight in your darkest times, and all you have to do is let them. Grieving Parents are some of the kindest, most wonderful giving people that I have ever met in my entire life. They understand that it's going to be hard for you to ask, so they're just going to show up. They're going to take up arms beside you, anyway.

All grieving parents need support, hope, and faith, but we go about getting it in different ways. So, whether it's in a church, whether you're religious, or whether you're just spiritual, sometimes just knowing that you're connected to other people, you're connected to something greater. You have to work with what you feel like at the moment and what works for you.

o **Professional Therapists and Counselors**

It's the same thing with professional therapy and counseling. It's very helpful for others because a therapist, a counselor, or a psychologist creates a safe space, so you can vent. For a lot of people, having an objective person whose opinion about you doesn't matter is safe, and it helps. When I need to vent, sometimes I go out and I yell at a tree. That's my safe space. The tree is non-judgmental.

o **Church Members**

Lexi loved hanging out with the youth group from church. It was a safe place for her, and it was a way to make her religion social, combining friendship with fellowship. She enjoyed her friends from high school. She enjoyed her cousins.

The same thing applies to grieving parents who find strength in groups of people with similar interests at different times. The more support, the more friends you have, the better.

o **Members of Non-Profit Organizations**

There is a wonderful national group called The Compassionate Friends. My friend Elgin, who is one of the first people I called after Lexi died, became very active in his local chapter. It's a place for parents and grandparents and siblings of deceased children to find people who understand, and you can talk to them about anything and everything. You can probably find a chapter pretty close to you wherever you live in the United States. People who attend those meetings have had experiences similar to yours and know something about your pain.

Compassionate Friends is mostly for grieving parents, but it's also support for family and siblings and friends. They understand that there are so many different people that need compassionate friends for one reason or another after the tragic loss in the family.

There are so many people from different walks of life who meet and vent and discuss their children's lives and the impact they had. I tried it and again, it was bunch of strangers. It didn't work for me, but I have seen it work for a lot of people. Even if you don't join, they have links to books or websites that can help you or other family members.

o **Members of the GrievingParentsClub.org**

I've also set up a new website at grievingparentsclub.org to help other Club members and their loved ones in ways that work for people with a personality more like mine, who don't find comfort in going to a group meeting with a bunch of strangers. There's nothing wrong with it, and talking with strangers is fine. Still, going in person and talking to people can be unnerving, and sometimes the anonymity of a blog or asking online questions can be a resource in and of itself. It's a very unique site, as I've yet to find anything like it out there. One thing that really worked for me and may help you is participating in a forum of caring Club members, where you can share your thoughts and feelings, speak your child's name, post pictures, and talk about your child and your relationship with them. Every day, we find different things that help us and different things that hurt us. I certainly don't have all the answers about what works and what doesn't work, but for other people, whether they're new or whether they've been in the Club for a long time, this website is a positive, non-judgmental place.

There's also a private Facebook group called The Grieving Parents Club where members can connect and support each other on social media. And, as always, I invite and encourage you and other Club members —especially the newest ones—to contact me directly to talk privately, if you like.

CHAPTER 8

KEEP MOVING

"Depression never hits a moving target."
– Barbara Ann Bovino

Each member of the Grieving Parents Club develops their own way of coping and healing, but there are certain things that many grieving parents do before and after the last damn bridge that seem to work better than most. This chapter is about those things.

I hope some of them work for you, too.

1. Help Others

I'm not really comfortable with having people help me, but I'm very comfortable with helping others. I do much better reaching out to others, just as I did when I comforted Lexi's friends at the funeral. I do better when I think about other people.

• Educate Children and Their Parents about the Club

I started talking to high school students, Driver's Ed classes, school assemblies, and even parents of Driver's Ed students in the fall of 2006. Within just a few months of Lexi's death, I was talking about how awesome she was, how amazing she was.

I wanted to tell them the story, and so my speeches and presentations can be anywhere from 10 minutes to an hour. I talk about choices behind the wheel. Lexi chose to speed. She chose not to wear her seat belt. She chose not to focus on driving; she became distracted, and choices have consequences. I talk about the fact that because of the choices Lexi made, my life is forever changed. The lives of my family members and those of her friends are changed as well. It was very hard on them.

I talk about having hopes and dreams. I tell them how she tried for two years to make the cheerleading squad, and how it's important to have goals. It's important to have dreams and never give up on them. I try to engage them and get them thinking about their hopes and dreams, and the only way they're going to achieve them is if they stay alive. That's why I do it—so no other parent ever has to go through what I go through. That's my big thing.

I must have given 100 speeches over the last ten years, maybe more. I even had the recent opportunity to speak in Idaho. It's always tough to talk to parents and groups of adults because that's when I have to focus on me and my choices. I remind them that the Driver's Ed teacher only has our children behind the wheel for about six hours, but they've been watching us drive since we put them in a car seat. Parents are the most important Driver's Ed instructors for their children, but how many of us consider that they notice our bad habits? They do as we do, not as we tell them to do. So, my speech to parents is basically the same one that I give to the students, but it has a different twist.

This is where some of the guilt comes in for me. I didn't always wear a seatbelt when Lexi was in the car with me, and I'm sure I exceeded the speed limit when I was in a hurry to get somewhere. Well, Lexi didn't learn those behaviors in Driver's Ed in school, so she had to pick them up somewhere else.

Before something happens that parents will forever regret, they have a chance to really talk to their teens; they have a chance with younger siblings to change their own behavior, to become a better example and a better role model as far as driving is concerned. I really try to get that across to them.

• Offer Scholarships or Awards

I wanted to give back to the high school that Lexi loved, so I started a scholarship in her memory. It's not a huge scholarship. I save a little money for students from Lexi's school who will be going to Parkland College, where I work. (This will be the 10th year I'm doing this. It started with the graduating seniors in 2007. They would have been a year older than Lexi.) I started with just $500 each. I picked two seniors who would be going to Parkland. I didn't look so much at their grades because Lexi's grades weren't tremendous. I do look at those who love the school, who are involved, and who maybe chose clubs and cheering. Those students who really demonstrate Lexi's spirit are the ones I consider for this scholarship. It's a rural school, so it is tough for some of the parents, especially with our state's economy.

It seemed natural to give out this award again during Lexi's graduating year, so the second year I did the scholarship, I gave away $2000 scholarships, just because I could. Recipients must be graduates from Saint Joseph-Ogden High School who go to Parkland College. Now, it's not so bad because I don't know these younger students, but I cover up the names so I can't show any favoritism.

• Give to Charity

I also try to help and love others in some ways. For example, at the yearly Fall Sports Banquet at Saint Joseph Ogden High School, the cheerleading squad chooses one person that never gives up, that doesn't have to be the center of attention, that's always helping people, and they are awarded The Lexi Barbour Spirit Award.

The Lexi Barbour Award for Football Cheerleading

Apparently, it's a big thing, and everybody wants it because it reflects what Lexi did. She didn't give up. She didn't quit. I wanted to give back to the cheer squad for being so important to Lexi and for continuing to remember her in this special way.

There are a lot of up-front costs for girls who make the cheerleading squad. Cheerleading camp is expensive, and including outfits and everything else, it's about $1000. I donated money to the cheer squad to help defray some or all of the camp cost which is about $350 a year. I know that not every parent can justify that cost, but I don't want money to keep another girl from achieving her dream of being a cheerleader. The coaches can use the money for that or for whatever else will help the girls. This year they will get a big tumbling mat—girls for years to come will be able to make good use of it.

I wish I could give more, but it adds up. I'm not wealthy by any means, but I'm comfortable, and it's important to me. It's just as important to me as saving for college education or donating to other charities.

- ## Support Fellow Club Members

I've been in the club for 10 years now, and I know how it feels. So, I reach out to other grieving parents, and I do it for free. I don't even take money from schools to travel. I don't think about money, but anytime I hear of a death that's similar to Lexi's, I try to make a point of going at least to the visitation and meeting the parents. I always have my business card, and I write my cell phone number on the back. I wait in line. I go up to them, and I give them a big hug. I try to get their contact information if it's somebody I know. Especially with new members to the Club, I make it a point to check in on them from time to time without being overbearing. I am only one person in the end.

New members of the Club almost always thank and compliment me for being so strong. They often say that they hope to be like me and keep their child's memory alive in the ways that I've been doing for Lexi. They also thank me for checking in on them. It's nothing big. I do it when I sense that somebody needs a virtual hug, virtual smile, something like that because I know that they do it for me when I'm down, too.

When I was in Idaho recently, I happened to meet a lady in the parking lot of a restaurant. We started chatting, and I had told her why I was in town and what I spoke about. She confided in me that her stepson had been killed in an accident 7 years prior. We showed each other pictures of our children, and then we hugged, laughed, and even cried together a bit. Members of the club are never strangers.

2. Laugh Again

You've got to laugh. In the early days you wonder, "Will I ever smile again? Will I ever laugh again? Is it okay to smile and laugh?" Starting off with a joke when I talk to high school students prepares me. It's easier since I know the tears will come. You cannot have a big belly laugh and be super happy and be angry or depressed at the same time.

I laugh at all kinds of things, including myself. We need humor to balance out the seriousness of life and death. It's yin and yang. Where there is darkness, there is light. You just have to find it.

Lexi was habitually happy and laughed all the time, but she was well-grounded too. Maybe she got some of that from me, but I was much more serious at her age. Fortunately, after a rough patch, I transformed into the "super-cool" mom who actually shared some interests with her teenage daughter. When Lexi was maybe 13 or 14, for example, I brought home the most recent Depeche Mode CD. She saw it and said, "Oh, thank you, thank you! I love Depeche Mode." I said, "This is for me." She couldn't believe it. I couldn't like the same music as her. I just said, "Seriously, Lexi, I've been listening to them since college." She wasn't pleased to hear that, but we got over it and pretty soon we were jamming together and joking about it.

3. Count Your Blessings and Choose to Be Happy

We *choose* to be happy or unhappy. So, every once in a while, choose to focus on what you do have as opposed to what you don't have. It's hard at times, especially shortly after the death of a child, but try your best to choose happiness anyway and develop a mindset of abundance and gratitude, not scarcity and bitterness.

Honestly, looking at Stasia's little two-and-a-half-year-old face with the grin and the curls saved me early on. She's amazing. First of all, she's a straight-A student, which is a proud mom moment, but she's also involved in things. She has such self-confidence, self-assuredness, and self-esteem, much more than I had at age 12. She is comfortable in her own skin. She's comfortable talking about Lexi; a lot of adults aren't, but that was kind of normal to her. She's funny, and her friends are funny. She doesn't have a lot of memories of Lexi simply because Lexi was older and was with friends a lot. She was so small when Lexi died, but I kept a lot of Lexi's things for her, including all of her CDs, some of her favorite outfits, her homecoming dresses, and all of her stuffed animals and beanie babies.

Ten years later, Stasia loves to put on one of Lexi's sweatshirts or read her books, or listen to her CDs because they have the same taste in music although Stasia has added a few recent ones to her repertoire. We found Lexi's original iPod about a month ago—I thought it had been in her car and was forever lost. Stasia squealed with delight when she saw that Lexi had her favorite bands on it, like Panic at the Disco, Green Day, and Fall Out Boy. Stasia also loves the same stupid silly TV shows as Lexi. It's amazing. She's sweet and kind and grinning. I am very grateful.

I come from a very close family. When there are six kids in a family, there are a lot of nieces and nephews to care for (I must have 16 of them), but I love being an aunt because, I have no guilt about spoiling them. As the aunt (Aunt Kiki), I love to spoil and play with them. In some small ways, it's bittersweet because I wish Lexi could get to know some of them, too. All these kids that have the same spirit as Lexi; it's just amazing.

I'm also grateful for some financial stability and know I can't take it for granted. So many people, especially in the state of Illinois, are going through a very tough time. I have a good job that doesn't just pay well, it's also a career. I love it. I don't dread getting up in the mornings and going to work. I love it. It energizes me because I'm talking to young people about topics I like: finance and economics. Then, over the last few years, I've been taking on more leadership roles in the college, and I was even asked to appear on local media to give my expert opinion. Business and finance is a passion of mine, and I love that they pay me to do this. I am very grateful, but because I have been blessed with a good job and benefits and good pay, I want to give back to other people. I remember growing up with an outhouse and a pump. We didn't even have running water. So I know what it's like to be poor.

I'm thankful to be in such good health, too. I can run a marathon. My closest sister has rheumatoid arthritis. She was a very athletic person, and it's been hard for her to live with the disease. I know other people that are going through health challenges, and I am grateful that if I had to have a joint that is giving me problems, it is my shoulder and not my knees. I am grateful that I can travel to different places and run races. It's easy to lose sight of that. It is so easy to dwell on the negative, but every single one of us has something positive to focus on if we choose to.

4. Live in the Present Moment

Learn to appreciate and live in the present moment. I know it's hard for new Club members to do, but you gain the capacity to do it in time. It took me a few years, but eventually you realize not to sweat the small stuff. Honestly, if Stasia doesn't make her bed or clean her room—of course, she does because she's the perfect child and her room is always spotless!—but if she doesn't pick up stuff, that is not something to throw a fit about. Pick your battles and live in the moment. Take a deep breath of fresh air and smell the flowers.

When you appreciate what you do have in life, it boosts your immune system. It helps you steel yourself for the next time that the waves of grief and emotion come.

5. Fight Back Your Way

I still have to fight. It's still the last 6.2 miles uphill. It's still a fight. It's still a struggle at times. But you have to fight. If you give up, you're done. How you choose to fight is up to you. There's no one-size-fits-all, but you have to help yourself by fighting back your way.

Since I crossed the Last Damn Bridge, and to a lesser extent long before that, I've used my talents and interests to cope, heal, and fight back against my grief and demons, and I've seen other Club members do the same. Do what's best for you, but it's likely that some of my methods will work for you. Choose the ones you like: talking about my child, the Club, and lessons learned; moving and exercising, especially running; indulging in certain things and activities, just for me; helping and loving others, especially new members of the Club and teenagers; doing certain things just for me; and counting my blessings, past and present.

• Talk It Out

Talking gives me strength. I talk for a living, and I love it. Talking allows me to communicate to people, to let them know, not only about Lexi and how awesome she was, but also a little about me. Whether it's talking to students in high school about teen safe driving or talking to other parents or reaching out, talking is a good outlet. It's venting. You're verbalizing your feelings and helping others.

I've been doing that, and it's very therapeutic for me. But I also get to talk about Lexi, and I get to introduce her to a whole new group of students and people who never got to meet her in person.

After teaching my class one day, a student came up and she tells me, "I just figured out who you are." She's been in class all semester. And I don't know if it's because I didn't have my glasses on that day or what. She tells me, "You spoke at Clifton Central High School last year. You told us about Lexi! I always wear my seat belt, and it didn't dawn on me today that you are Lexi's mom. You were just amazing!" And this was a year later. I told her, "Thank you. You have just made my day." I began to tear up. I see the impact that I make on the faces of the students when I'm there, but then I wonder as weeks and months and years go by, do they still retain Lexi's story? Does it impact their behavior? Do they change their driving behavior? And she confirmed this.

I'm just the medium. But Lexi is still making people happy. She's still impacting people's lives for the better. That is awesome. It absolutely made my day.

• **Move!**

Grief is a huge stressor. Even when you're not outwardly crying or sad, grief itself is a huge stressor. It causes psychological, mental, and physiological effects.

So, if you let yourself get run down, if you're not resting, if you're not eating right, if you're not hydrating, if you're not moving, get out. Let your endorphins, adrenaline, and the fresh air combine to combat your sadness, especially after a horrible winter.

It doesn't matter what you do, as long as you're moving, because depression can't hit you if you are. Go to a movie. Get a manicure. Get a pedicure. Do something for you; if you don't take care of yourself and your immune system gets depleted, you can't be there for anybody else. Since that is the case, it's not selfish.

If I can do it, so can you. I was a bookworm. After Lexi had been gone for five years, I had a lot of people suggesting I try these mud runs, these obstacle course runs. They said they were a lot of fun. They told me that you cannot take yourself seriously and you cannot be depressed if you're completely covered in mud and you're jumping over fire. But I replied, "I'm not a runner. I've never run. I don't think my knees can handle it." And they came back with a simple, "It's fun." I would see pictures. I just thought, "That looks like fun. That looks just crazy, seriously."

I started with a simple free couch to 5K app for my phone, and I followed it. During those early days of jogging for 1 minute and walking for 4 minutes, I remember thinking, "Will this one minute of jogging ever end?" And pretty soon, you begin to build. Put one foot in front of the other. You build your endurance, and suddenly, my knees didn't hurt. My very first race ever was a warrior dash. I was all muddy, and I had the best time of my life. You have to laugh at yourself as you're sliding down muddy hills. You can't keep it together. It's okay to laugh.

It's kind of the same thing. I can have fun and laugh. So, I did a bunch more. I couldn't do the yoga meditation because my mind was going too fast, but I could just kind of be in the moment with the running. I found it was good not just physically, but mentally because it was calming me down. I wasn't thinking about how sad I was and how miserable and unfair life was, so that absolutely worked for me.

Now, physically I can do a lot more. I just feel better. I think if you feel better physically, that helps your disposition and your energy levels. It worked for me. Gardening works for some people. Bike riding works, too. Going to the lake is the same thing. But all these activities have two things in common: fresh air and moving.

When Stasia was young, I would just go to the gym, or maybe do a step aerobics class. It didn't work as well. So, then I decided, "I'm going to try this program called P90X at home," and that was a fast no (although I did finish it much later on). Then I tried this program called Insanity at home, and I believed that I could do this. I lost weight. I lost body fat. I became stronger. My blood pressure went down. My cholesterol went down. I had more energy. I looked better. I didn't look like I was pale and drawn. That gave me the confidence to try running. I ran my first marathon on November 1, 2015, in New York City. This is the world's biggest marathon. If you're going to do one, it may as well be the biggest. I'd done half marathons, but that was my very first marathon.

I was running on sheer determination. When I got past the 17-mile mark in New York City, I bawled. I thought, if I can make it this far, I can make it. It took me 6 hours, but I crossed the finish line. You have to have goals. You need something to shoot for. I had a goal and, by golly, it took me 6 hours, but I finished and I got that medal.

Never give up!!

- ## Indulge and Take Risks

The world won't stop turning if you take some time for yourself once in a while and do certain things just for you.

o **Read All About It**

Go read a book if you want. Lock yourself in a room and tell your other kids unless the house is burning down, I don't want to hear anybody say "Mom" for at least five minutes.

o **Get Some Ink**

A few months after Lexi died, I did something else really crazy. I honestly don't know why, because I had always been the kind of person who was a little judgmental about women who had tattoos. But I was feeling the way I felt when Lexi was in the hospital and I got my navel pierced. I decided to get a tattoo.

I went to the same place that had done my piercing a few months earlier, and I told them everything that had happened in my life after they had last seen me. I told them about a little idea I had for a tattoo. They were very kind and helped me design it. I had a little scrap of paper that had Lexi's signature in cursive on it, and so I have a red heart on my hip. It has "Lexi" written in as close to their cursive signature as they can.

It wasn't that bad. It wasn't painful, but just like the piercing, it was rather cathartic. My whole attitude about tattoos changed. It was very discreet. It had meaning to me, and it's one of those things that no matter how old I get, it's never going to change. Then I found out that my mom, a couple weeks later, got the yellow rose of Texas. She was 63 years old at the time. My tattoo is discreet. Not hers. If she takes off her jacket, it's right there on her arm. It was healing. This is something that has deep meaning. In the years since, tons of parents get memorial remembrance tattoos. They choose something that means something to them. But it's kind of addictive.

That first Christmas my family decided we were all going to go to a different city in a different state; so, the first Christmas without Lexi and my granddad, Mom and I were in Austin, Texas, comparing tattoos.

We spent two Christmases at this vacation town in Austin as we tried to get ourselves together before having Christmas back at my parent's house in Fort Worth, Texas. The day after Christmas 2008, mom and I went to a really bad part of Fort Worth together; we went to her tattoo parlor and got mom and daughter tattoos.

I got a butterfly on the back of my shoulder blade. It's small, discreet and colorful. It has maroon and blue—Lexi's high school colors. The antennae make a cursive L, just like her signature. Mom basically had them add Lexi Jane. My mom has gone tattoo crazy now. So, it's crazy. But a lot of people do it.

o **Perform (in a Play)**

Unless it was a very close group of friends or family, I wasn't really that outgoing growing up. I preferred to have my head in a book. I didn't get involved in drama club or anything like that.

A year after Lexi died August of 2007, I'd had a really bad time. Well-meaning people had said very hurtful things. One in particular, a leader in the church, an elder and his wife had said, "Sorry you're having a really hard time getting over the death of your daughter. You need to move on, get over it and get back to church."

So, I heard that Parkland College, where I teach and where I work, was having auditions for *To Kill a Mockingbird*. This was one of my favorite books as a child, and I decided that I wouldn't get a role, but it would feel good just to audition. I needed to get out of the house.

So, I went and auditioned, and there was a very small role of the crazy neighbor Miss Stephanie, and I thought, "Well, I've got the Southern accent down, so I can do this." I read, and then the director said, "No, I want you to read this other role, Miss Maudie."

No. I remember Miss Maudie from the book. She's too big of a role. I went ahead and read for her with my Southern accent. The director told me, "Okay, you need to speed up." I replied, "Excuse me, do you want Southern or do you want fast?" Two days later, I got Miss Maudie. I had more lines than Atticus Finch had. I was the narrator basically for the whole thing. I thought that the director was out of her ever-loving mind.

But, I fell in love with acting. I discovered a talent. I met people. I got to play dress up and pretend. It was like Halloween, which is my favorite holiday. I got to be somebody else. I got to live out one of my favorite childhood books. Books can take you anywhere, but actually getting to immerse yourself in one of your favorite characters was a completely different experience. This was awesome because when I was acting, I didn't have to think about my life.

I have been doing community theater ever since. I was just cast in another show. I'm going to get to pretend at a very important time. School will be out soon. If I don't have something before June 28th, I tend to get a little down. One of my coping mechanisms is to keep busy with positive things. So this is perfect. I get to pretend. Play dress up. It's set in the 1980s, so we're going with big hair and kooky wild clothes. I caught the acting bug. What can I say? I love Community Theater. I love live theater. You never know what you're going to get.

It can be scary stepping out of your comfort zone, but being a member of the Grieving Parents Club is liberating in some ways. I'm not scared of anything because the worst thing that could ever possibly happen to me has already happened. I'm still standing. It's very liberating in that aspect, but it's also because I'm a new person. The day Lexi died, the old Kelly disappeared. Things that I got comfortable with, things that I thought I was good at—the old Kelly. I kept trying new things because it's a new me.

I may be good or I may suck, but I give the new me permission to try things.

People worry about public speaking because they wonder if people are going to laugh at them. Honestly, that is not the worst thing that can happen to you. And if you take control, and you get into a funny role or you introduce appropriate timely humor into a speech, then you're taking back control. And if people laugh, that's okay.

You get your priorities straight. It's your new life. It's a clean slate. You get to decide. Once you've gone through this, again, you get to decide. The old Kelly, my parents, my surroundings, early childhood and things like that, that really formed me. The new Kelly gets to pick. If I want to go to New York City and run 26 miles by myself, I'm going to do it. I'm going to have fun. I'm going to try it. I may fall. I may fail. I may not do it. But I'm going to go try it. I'm going to have fun, and I'm going to enjoy it.

o **Write – or Speak – a Book**

Becoming a member of the Club also led to this book. It led me to reach out to my friend, Joe Bovino of Bestseller in You Publishing (BestsellerInYou.com), who encouraged me to *speak* this book into existence. This is scary for me because even though I like to talk and communicate, I'm a very private person who doesn't open up easily to strangers about personal matters. That was very scary, and there were times early on when I thought, "Screw it, I can't do this," but the more I thought about it, the more I realized that I *can* absolutely do it. I can open up, tell my story, talk about my feelings, screw-ups, and all the rest.

It's very liberating to know that the absolute worst thing, the thing that every parent fears, has happened, and I'm still standing. I'm doing more than just functioning. I'm making a difference. I'm making an impact, so everything else that I could possibly be afraid of is nothing. I can totally handle it.

There were times when I wanted to quit. It was sad and scary at times for a private person like me to open up about my deepest darkest fears, thoughts, anger, and darkness, but it definitely wasn't the scariest or worst thing that's ever happened to me. And, now that it's over, I'm glad I jumped in and seized the opportunity to tell my story and help others!

CONCLUSION

"From a small seed a mighty trunk may grow."

- AESCHYLUS

Thank you for listening to my story… a grieving parent's story.

If I were to sum up what this book is about, it's that millions of parents are living their normal lives. Right now they're sitting in their homes, or they're sitting at work. They're making plans with their kids. They're planning summer vacations. Kids may be getting ready to graduate from high school or to go to prom, or parents are getting them ready for kindergarten and grade school. They're looking forward to spending time watching their children grow up and achieve things and live life to the fullest. But at some point, some of those millions of parents are going to find themselves exactly in my spot: the same darkness, the same daze, the same anger, wondering exactly how they will find the way back to themselves after their child's death.

They're going to ask, in their own way, "Why? What happened? Why did this happen to my child?" It's hard to know what to do when it first happens because you're in that daze. You're still trying to process that this isn't a dream, that this is reality. Very early on, a lot of parents are going to question: "Why should I even bother going on? How can I go on? How can I live life? Is it wrong to smile? Will I ever be happy again? Will I ever find joy? Am I ever going to have good days again? Should I even bother?" This book is really meant to give hope, support, and encouragement, and help these parents see that you absolutely can go on.

It's not always the easiest journey, but you can go on; you don't have to go it alone, and you can find some kind of meaning. Most importantly, you can be the continuing voice of your child. I'm Lexi's voice now. It's up to me to make sure that people know about her smile and her friendliness and her joy of life.

The main points of the book deal with questions that parents may have, as well as feelings and sometimes unexpected struggles that newly bereaved parents inevitably go through. This book offers a look at what has worked for me, and what has worked for others in the Grieving Parents Club.

This book doesn't offer a one-size-fits-all solution because it doesn't exist. (If it did, I would gladly share it with you and adopt it myself.) It contains tips, suggestions, and things that worked for me.

There are many wonderful groups and organizations and people that readers can go to learn more, whether they're grieving parents or friends or family that want to be able to help. *The Compassionate Friends* is a national group that often has local chapters in different towns and cities, and they're great. You can check in your community to see if there's a chapter. Churches are an invaluable resource as well. They either offer grief counseling or know the direction to point you in. You don't have to be a member; they will hold grief counseling, not just for parents who have lost children but for people who have lost spouses or suffered similar losses. Check with local hospitals. They have great advice. They don't provide actual counseling, but they certainly have networks, and they have the resources.

I've never been one to join in on a conversation with strangers about something so personal. However, for some, anonymity can be very freeing. It can allow you to open up without fear of judgment. When you meet in person or when you're with most of the traditional social media, they know something about you. It doesn't work for everybody. Some people don't mind. I don't mind people knowing once I've kind of tested the waters and felt them out.

I know there are probably a lot of grieving parents out there who are like me in this regard. What is out there is wonderful, but what is out there, as far as being able to communicate with grieving parents, isn't enough at times, so I'm hoping that this will add to the repertoire of things that are out there. You can never have too much help. helpful.

No matter how our children died, it doesn't make it easier. There's no time limit on grief. There's no right or wrong way to grieve. Time does not heal the wound that you get when you lose a child or when you have to bury your child, but gradually, time does softens the edges. You learn how to put bandages on when you need to. You learn to live with the pain and the new normal. In a way, you're taking control back of whatever pieces of your life you can. Instead of letting the grief and the pain and the anger control you, you find strength. You can take your life back.

If what is out there doesn't fit you at the time, that's okay. Things that are out there didn't fit me at various stages either, and that's one of the reasons I wanted to create GrievingParentsClub.org. My desire is not to replace all the wonderful organizations that are out there but to build a community. It is something that works for me with my personality, and I invite you to join me and other grieving parents as we survive, cope, and heal—together.

There's no guarantee, but long-term members of the Club like me have been doing this a while, and we've learned what works for us, for our lives, for our personalities, and what works for others. We have some tips. It helps if you have different choices to try. Learn from our mistakes, but also learn from our successes. Really, it takes new grieving parents through the various stages that you have to follow to make your way out of that darkness. When you first land in the Grieving Parents Club, that alternate universe, it's very dark, like going through a maze. And if you take the wrong route, there's a wall. Sometimes, you have to backtrack, but there's a way out—not out of the Grieving Parents Club, but out of the darkness to find the light, so you can breathe again.

There are a lot of us who have been in this club for a long time, and we can help. I was always taught that you have a talent, and you need to share it. That's the best way to help people. Sometimes, your talent can be giving a hug or being a shoulder to cry on. Sometimes, it can be talking. Sometimes, it can be networking. Sometimes, it can be making people laugh.

I'm about educating and informing people, whether it's in an academic situation, teaching college students about business and finance and economics, or talking about my daughter. The thing I have learned through teaching is that there is no single answer to a solution. Everyone learns differently. Just as when I talk to grieving parents, we all cope differently. Communication is paying attention and using what works, and if you don't have what works, helping people find the resources that will work. When I talk to high school students, which I've done about safe driving and making choices, I'm trying to educate and inform them. No matter what I do, I am a communicator, informer and educator.

As much as we don't want to be in the Club, we still learn from those who are. I learn from people who are new to the Club because they're doing things that help them that didn't occur to me at the time. I'm learning every day. I'm learning how I react to things. I'm learning new things that set me off so that the next time they occur, I can kind of prepare myself. I'm learning every day, and the more people unfortunately that are in the Club, the more I learn, the more we all learn.

Every time I hear a teenager is killed in a car wreck, I get sick. I mean physically and mentally sick. Talk about a wave. First, there's the flood of dread, and then I just become a zombie; it comes back. I hate that feeling. The main reason I give speeches is for other people to become better informed and supported, but I also do it for me, because I don't want that feeling every time I hear a teenager died in a car wreck.

If you need advice about how to cope with losing a child, or you know someone who lost a child and you aren't sure on how to support them properly, you can reach out to me directly anytime at kelly@grievingparentsclub.org. And I cordially invite you to join me and other members of the Club at our new website at www.GrievingParentsClub.org and our new, private Facebook group for The Grieving Parents Club.

Thanks again for listening. Remember… you are NOT alone in your journey.

ACKNOWLEDGMENTS

This book has been a dream of mine for many years, but I never thought it would become a reality.

Thank you to my beloved family and friends for being there for me since my painful initiation into the Grieving Parents Club more than ten years ago. I couldn't have made it this far or finished this book without your unconditional love and support. There are too many of you to thank individually without neglecting to mention someone, but special thanks to my husband Chris, adorable daughter Stasia, mom and dad, brothers and sisters, nieces and nephews (who continue to remember their sweet cousin, Lexi), and my YaYa Sisters – Kelly, Julie, & Mynda. I love you all very much.

As always, my love and gratitude also extend to other members of the Club, including but not limited to the parents of Brittany, Nicholas, Chason, James Lee, Cady, Melanie, Alena, Brycen, Danielle, Jennifer, J.J. and Jackie, Jared, Greg, Danny, Spencer, Mason, Sophia, Jordan, and LeToya, and all of our beautiful children.

And, finally, a very special thank-you to my friend Joe Bovino at Bestseller in You Publishing (BestsellerInYou.com) for his guidance, tireless work and encouragement. His easy 3-step writing and publishing process made this book possible and a dream come true, especially during the hard times when I didn't think I could continue telling the story.

CREDITS

EDITING & PROOFREADING

Diane Chesson, Ph.D, MBA
www.drdianechesson.com; diane.chesson@gmail.com.

Sara Bernhardt
https://www.upwork.com/freelancers/_~01ad94e42e909ba8b7/;
singinsara3@gmail.com.

Joe Bovino
www.bestsellerinyou.com;
joe@bestsellerinyou.com.

BOOK DESIGN & LAYOUT

www.iPublicidades.com

CPSIA information can be obtained
at www.ICGtesting.com
Printed in the USA
LVHW072133060322
712777LV00025B/588